30 Ideas

THE IDEAS OF SUCCESSFUL JOB SEARCH

**Practical and easy-to-use tips
for the modern job search.**

•••

Includes advice on:
creating a job search strategy
maintaining a positive mindset
building a career networking plan
and much, much more!

Tim Tyrell-Smith

Cover design and layout: Merlina Design
http://merlinadesign.com

Creator, Blogger, Speaker at Tim's Strategy™

Tim Tyrell-Smith is a 22 year veteran consumer packaged goods marketing executive. Passionate about ideas and strategy, Tim lives with his wife and 3 children in Mission Viejo, California.

Contents

Introduction

In 2007, I became officially unemployed (in between) for the first time in my career. It was joyful, stressful, freeing, exciting and frustrating all at the same time. And, in some ways, I needed to make a game of it.

To find unique analogies that I could use to maintain a positive and confident psychology. You see, there is something very stimulating about being on the job hunt. You get to test your skills against many others and in front of a great variety of hiring managers. Where else do we really get to compete in life anymore?

Plate spinning as the first analogy for job search, career and life

The act of plate spinning was the first analogy I identified because its focus was on efficiency – the best, most productive use of time spent. And it led to the original name I used for the blog and website. You see, I found during my own search that people were tapping into too few resources and using them up beyond their usefulness. And I think we have opportunities to apply this idea broadly throughout life.

I originally called it "spin strategy"

Building this community is an act of thanks to all who helped me during my own search. To get started, I created a name and a logo (after all, I'm in marketing) and started to share the idea with a few friends. I then created a set of tools to help job seekers identify and determine how best to use their network – all based initially on the analogy of plate spinning. As the concept matured and caught on, job seekers wanted more than just a concept or a tool. They wanted a broad menu of resources so I started to blog and began to create free downloads to support the job search. And plate spinning became just one of many ideas to share.

Then I made some changes . . .

About 15 months into creating the concept, I decided to make a change. To re-jigger things a bit. So I re-named the blog and combined it with the website. It became Tim's Strategy. After all, it did originate in my head, right? And every day I write or build a new tool, the strategy gets more complete. So now I am working on ways to pull it all together. There are ebooks, an eworkbook, and a new hard cover book in process that I hope to get published. But in reality, the content is not mine alone. Like anything that is created from experience, it is never one person's strategy alone. But it's mostly mine!

It's A Competitive Market

But, let's be clear. Tim's Strategy is still a very young concept. I hope it will become a great resource for lots of people. But today it is an interesting idea waiting for you to share it with others. There are a lot of great resources out there on the web to career and personal development. I only hope Tim's Strategy can add to the quality content available and do so in a fun and inventive way.

So, what's next?

I continue to write on the blog and look for new ways to bring this concept to life. We may do a few national webinars or seminars in Southern California to get away from the computer, meet you and share our ideas in a more personal way. Looking for a speaker? Let me know!

The rest? Well, that's up to you.

I hope you enjoy this book. It represents the best of the blog since its inception. Now you might be asking: what's the value of this book when much of the information is already out on the blog? Well, I've re-edited some of the blogs, organized them into three critical sections and I'll tell you, it is really difficult to find content that is two months old. And older content might be just what you need… right now!

So I've organized the book around three key areas. After writing for 15 months and completing 231 posts, these are the three big ideas. The three things you have to get right in order to succeed in job search. They are:

- Job Search Strategy
- The Psychology of Successful Job Search
- Smart Networking

Each section includes 10 chapters to help you succeed in each critical area. And this new 2010 edition includes 2 bonus chapters!

These are ideas. Easy to read and easy to implement. And you can start tomorrow.

I am so grateful to share these ideas with you!

Now it's your turn… who can you share these ideas with? Feel free to share this book with anyone in transition, out-of-work or unhappy in their current job. It may be just the thing they need!

Good luck out there!
Tim Tyrell-Smith
November 2010
Oh, and send me a note with your feedback. Would you?

Job Search
Strategy

1

Do You Have A Job Search Strategy Or Are You Just Spinning?

Memories of the Big Top

When I was a kid I used to love the circus act of plate spinning - all those plates and only one person keeping them afloat! The beauty of it, of course, is the efficiency of only re-spinning the plate when it starts to slow down.

The Analogy for Job Search

As I was in the middle of a recent job transition, plate spinning struck me as a compelling analogy for job search. So I started to think about plate spinning as it related to my own efforts to find that perfect next position. In the analogy, each plate represents the different sources of information or resources used to network (I call them micro networks). How many plates was I spinning and how often was I going back to each one?

How Was I Doing?

After a quick review, I found that I had too few plates spinning and was re-spinning the same ones way too often. Sound familiar? I was inefficient by definition! I also found that I had my favorite plates, many of which were really fun to spin but were either not very effective or didn't respond to extra spinning. Here were my core plates: recruiters, job search engines, and on-line networking groups.

If you are like me at all, you love sites like Linkedin®, The Ladders®, Monster® and RiteSite®. The visits are highly rewarding for those of us who need immediate gratification. They also play a clear and important role in maintaining a wide scope in your search effort. The reality is that there are many more plates out there to spin. And, as you might expect, each has its own value.

Being out of work in an uncertain economy can be stressful and frustrating. Being out of work without a strategy is just downright silly. Yet most people I met who were in transition did not have a specific plan. There was outward confidence, activity, pride, but often not much else. So what does a job search strategy look like and how do I get one?

So what makes sense is a new, efficiency-based job search strategy. It helps place the right efforts against the right resources to maximize the return in job search. Here's how it works:

1. IDENTIFY your plates
These are basically all of the micro networks that make up your overall network (e.g. a recruiter or an old college friend). By identifying each micro network you can then begin the process of comparing the relative value of each one and how often each should be resourced or "spun".

2. VALUE your plates

Each plate gets a value based on specific criteria. Once valued, your plates are ranked giving you a real sense of where you should be spending your time.

3. MEASURE your spinning stick

How open is this micro network to helping you? You can do this by measuring your spinning stick. It shows the relative distance between you and your micro network. In plate spinning a shorter stick is less awkward to work with and in this strategy it suggests a closer relationship to your network - one you can tap into more deeply and more often.

4. CHOOSE a spin cycle for each plate

Based on the value and closeness of each network, you can decide how often to spin each plate. Once the analysis is complete you can have confidence in a specific plan to make sure your networks know that you are looking and are reminded about your skills and targets.

5. KEEP a log

Can you remember the last time you e-mailed that recruiter? Do you remember what feedback each of your networks provided last time you spoke? A log tracks every contact with your micro networks allowing you to measure the ongoing value and return as time goes on. So, ask yourself, do you have a strategy or are you just spinning?

2

Job Search Advice.
It's The Same Stuff We
Learned As Kids.

Sorry if this job search advice sounds preachy. I don't mean it that way. If it weren't for the people who break a few key rules, this article would not be necessary.

But because I want you to succeed and because I realize that all of us are prone to mistakes and narcissistic behavior during a search, here are some things to remember.

1. Job search can be stressful but it's not the end of the world.

When I was a few years younger (OK, I was 28) and had just become a husband, I shared a feeling with a new uncle in-law. "Uncle Mike", I said, "I'm stressed." Well, Uncle Mike has lived a bit. A tough rugby player (in his day) from England. His response? He laughed. It turns out that I had a bit to learn about stress. My newly married stress was the tip of the iceberg. My point? Being out of work is a challenging time but it is not something that should alter who you are or how you carry yourself socially or during interviews. Take the long view and use the stress as a motivator.

2. Let's be honest.

It can be tempting to stretch the truth. People do it all the time on resumes, in cover letters, during networking events and, painfully, in interviews. Why painfully? Because it does more damage than good - especially in the long term. In a past article, I spoke about not disguising your true self. So, review your resume and, yes, make sure you are your biggest cheerleader. But, don't give yourself credit for things you didn't do or awards you didn't earn. Those are likely not what you will be hired for anyway.

3. Try a little kindness along the way.

During your job search, there will be plenty of people to step on or walk over. Folks who have become stuck and need a fresh perspective, a leg up or some friendly advice. But, you might say, "who am I to deliver that value? I'm in the same boat!" In my opinion you are uniquely qualified for just that reason. Your advice comes from recent experience and your leads come from qualified recruiters or hiring managers. If you want to help someone, they are easy to find at a networking event. Look for the deer in the headlights people over by the bar. Want an easy way to help? Download the *Watchlyst*™ from my free tools page and easily track the job objectives of those people in your network.

4. R-E-S-P-E-C-T.

Respect the time of hiring managers and recruiters. You do this by realizing that they have full-time jobs along with plenty of other candidates to review. Get your candidacy strongly placed in front of them and then back off. Daily e-mails to check your status are not going to get you in any sooner. Respect the reputation of your network. If someone has provided a lead to you, please don't abuse it. And please don't suggest that you have a stronger relationship with this person then you actually enjoy. Respect fellow job seekers by giving them the benefit of your experience - even if you are 10 years their senior. You never know where that next lead will come from, right?

So, these are four things I learned early on in life. Sometimes we all need a reminder to follow them again at certain times. And job search is a great time to do so.

What lessons do you follow? And what rules do you see being broken out there?

3

Warning!
This Job Search Is
Under Construction.

During my job search back in 2007 there were days when I felt I needed a man with a stop sign out in front of my house. He was there to direct traffic around my house but, more directly, around the constantly changing nature of my job search.

You see, I learned a lot in 2007. And just because I am writing about my experiences now does not mean I was an expert back then. I made mistakes. My expertise has grown as a result of my writing, my networking and the testing of ideas with people who are in the middle of their own job search.

You may know there are two different types of construction. The kind that happens in most U.S. cities and the kind that happens in Chicago. If you have ever travelled to Chicago or surrounding areas, you will have heard the phrase: "There are two seasons in Chicago. Winter and Construction." So what does the traffic look like around your house?

To kick off your effort, you need to spend significant time up front on your job search strategy. Whether you are doing a re-paving, adding a lane or building a bridge, those first 2-4 weeks are critical.

Not only do they set the urgency and importance of your effort, but they also establish your early credentials.

All those early e-mails and networking meetings will include your most trusted and reliable contacts. Don't ruin the unique opportunity to re-establish yourself with poorly constructed marketing materials.

So there is the up-front effort that we can all agree is critical. What then? Well, you can't just sit still with your materials in a changing market, can you? Isn't that job search suicide? Actually I think you can.

- *Once you have established your job search objectives.*
- *Once you have confirmed your special qualities, your measurable successes and your relevant qualifications.*
- *Once you have built a complete set of marketing materials for yourself.*

Then you can go out and take action with these tools. As a very astute person said on my *LinkedIn group,* you can go get some "Face Time!" All the preparation in the world won't do anything for you without brilliant execution. Go out and meet the key people that need to see your skills and personality proven - in person.

You won't get a job offer over the phone. I've heard stories of this happening, but I don't believe it.

Interviews and job offers come when you make an impact on someone. Either the hiring manager directly or someone who knows him or her and says to them. "Wow, you have to meet this person".

So...

Pick a point within the first 2-4 weeks where you are done with the writing, tweaking and re-jiggering of your resume, cover letter and such. That point should become obvious as your changes get very insignificant. You can always come back and adjust your materials as needed due to market changes or when target company opportunities require a special version.

But, for the most part, once you figure out who you are, what you are good at and where you'd like to focus your talents, stop clowning around.

OK, sure, but what's wrong with making a few changes each week? Honestly, no one will likely even notice that you made the changes. You have now left Bigpicture city and are traveling on the Wasteoftime Expressway. Your efforts will be about as efficient as four guys in orange vests standing around an open ditch. Oh, and if you are always under construction, you'll probably sound like it in your interviews.

So... Build your strategy. Create materials to support it. Execute.

And stop re-digging the same holes for yourself. Get out there and get something new started.

4

Laid Off - Like a Tornado

I'm lucky in a number of ways.

One way is that I get to meet a lot of smart people through authoring the Tim's Strategy blog. Many meetings are by phone. Not ideal in many cases but the emotions come across regardless. And, because we are new in our relationship, people are more open in sharing the details of their situation.

The most compelling discussions are with people who need help after a layoff - especially if you have the opportunity to speak with them within days or weeks of the lay off. So I was thinking today that the experience of being laid off is like experiencing a tornado.

Not one that leaves physical destruction of course, but there are many similarities both in terms of the immediate impact and the clean up and re-building that begins once the dust settles.

1. With most lay-offs you get very little notice. The sudden, unanticipated news can shake you. There is frustration due to the often random nature of the decision. Why me? Why now? What will I do?

2. Like tornados, job layoffs tend to come as local events. Hitting a community or a small division of a big company. A plant shutdown is a good example. So you know a lot of other people affected by the event and have a group of folks now in a need to re-group.

3. As the winds die down, the community comes out to see what happened. Is everyone OK? In the case of layoffs, however, the true nature of most company relationships are laid bare. Those affected are often left to fend for themselves with little help from fellow employees and a package of benefits from the company that never feels quite enough.

4. Then comes the sorting through process. Trying to figure out what you lost and what can be salvaged. A feeling of loss. After a layoff, there are many questions regarding your benefits, how long they last and what needs to be done to get them activated. Many good companies provide help with activation of these benefits and even provide some ongoing support. Either directly or through out placement. Unlike the Red Cross, there are some out placement firms out there offering only surface value.

5. The important re-building process then begins. Mentally and physically you need to prepare for your next role in the work world. Depending on your lay-off situation, it can either be psychologically damaging or a welcome relief (the latter tends to be something that is only realized months later). For the former, there is real healing that needs to happen. One needs to shift from focusing on the old job to planning for the new one.

So how do you re-build after a lay-off?

1. KNOW YOUR BENEFITS

Sit with your spouse ASAP and make sure you are both clear on what benefits you have and don't have along with roughing out an early budget. Do not assume (especially if the lost income was the only one in the family) that a new job will be found quickly. Optimism is great in job search as it is important to believe in yourself.

That the next job is just around the corner. But please don't build a financial plan that assumes a quick end to the job search.

2. BUILD YOUR STRATEGY

Start with your job objectives. What are you looking for in your next job? Set your targets: title, industry, companies, function, geography, benefits. Who will you tap to communicate these objectives? What role will recruiters play? How will you use the job search sites? Where will you pay for services (paid search, career coach, etc) vs. going it alone? What guiding principles will steer your time and energy each day?

3. PREPARE YOUR PERSONAL MARKETING MATERIALS

Your personal marketing materials speak for you in your absence. They must be well written and precise. They must tell your story in a meaningful way. In addition to your resume (max 2 pages), you need a way to introduce yourself. Sometimes that is a cover letter. At networking events that can be a one-sheet like the *SoloSheet*™ You also need ways to leave people with a professional impression. Do you have a business card that reminds people of your job objectives and positions you well for that ideal job? Are your references in order? Are they ready and willing to share meaningful accomplishments that will be relevant to the hiring company?

4. TELL THE WORLD

Do not be shy with this one. Done correctly, sharing your job search objectives with friends, family, former co-workers, the check-out lady at the grocery store, etc is vital. I say correctly because there are good and bad ways to spread the word. Make sure your job objectives are clear and memorable. People can only help you if you leave them with a tangible memory. If not, you'll get back very little.

5. NETWORK LIKE CRAZY

Effective job search includes not only communicating with your current circle, but, more important is to reach out to a larger crowd. Preferably made up of people in your industry. Join an industry association. Go to seminars or events where people who hire will attend.

6. TAKE TIME FOR YOU

Lay-offs can be painful. You can feel wronged or cheated. Angry. Those are common emotions. Taking time for you is therapeutic to help heal those wounds and, more important, can get you back in the right frame of mind to interview. Once you begin interviewing, no one wants to hear your frustrations. They want to hear about your ability to have a positive impact on their company. And you can't communicate that with a chip on your shoulder.

7. GET IN SHAPE AND EAT RIGHT

What to do with your extra time? Get fit. You'll feel better, look better and, as an extra benefit, your interview suit won't be quite as snug!

8. SHOW PATIENCE

The job search process takes time. Impatience doesn't make it go any faster. Build your strategy and give it time to play out. Patience comes across as cool and confident - especially across a desk during an interview. It also prevents any nagging of recruiters or hiring managers during the process. If you act like you have a lot going on, you are more interesting than someone who clearly only has eyes for one opportunity. Don't seem desperate - even if you feel that way some days.

9. INTERVIEW AS MUCH AS POSSIBLE

Interviewing is good for you. Practice interviewing is great preparation for the important ones down the road. The more you put yourself into a face-to-face discussion, the more comfortable and polished you will be when it counts. So, find jobs to interview for even if they are not ideal. Give it your best. Get an offer and you can take that confidence with you.

10. A TEACHABLE MOMENT

If this was your first lay-off or your first time out of work in your career, go look yourself in the mirror and say this: "Never again". Never again will I avoid networking because I didn't NEED to at the time. It is so easy to network while working. It takes time and focus, yes. But, boy does it pay off when you really need it. Instead of starting from scratch, you have a whole crew of people ready to help you clean up and re-build. Many of whom you helped find a job over the past few years.

So, think about it.

What was your lay-off experience like? Is this a reasonable analogy? If not, what did it feel like to you?

5

10 Reasons You Should Regularly Read A Job Search Blog

Now, coming from a guy who regularly writes a job search blog, you might find this article a bit self-serving. And, if I'm honest, you're probably right. I would love it if you would regularly read my blog.

You might also be concerned about my intentions. "He's probably trying to increase his traffic." Got me again. I am.

But where you may not have me is in my purpose. If you look around the site, you'll notice something. Figure it out? No banner ads. Nope. None.

Now, before I get all high and mighty on you, there have been ads on the blog before. Early on I tested them. But I have removed them all and I think the blog looks a lot better. Cleaner.

So, back to the purpose. My purpose here is to give back. To the community that helped me during my job search back in late 2007. For 5 months I toiled just like you. But perhaps unlike you, I kept notes. I kept notes on every aspect. I also found unique ways (analogies) to think through my strategy. And I built one. And now I'm sharing it all with you.

So, since that is all out of the way, shall we get back to the 10 reasons?

1. You Get New Ideas

When I first started to write the blog my raw material was my ideas. Not having formal training as a career coach or a professional resume writer, I used my experiences as a hiring manager, job seeker and marketer. I've been an idea guy since birth and love finding new ways to get a thought across to people. So, why do you need ideas? Because life in job search can get monotonous. And new ideas can put some pep back in your engine at just the right time.

2. You Meet A Friend

Can you really make friends with a blogger? Aren't they reclusive people who abhor shaving and avoid most in-person or phone contact? Gosh, I don't know! But I'll tell you that's not me. Ask the people on the Linkedin Group who send me a note. To my own peril (lack of sleep), I get back to everyone and see how/if I can help. So, yes, if you need a friend on some days when things aren't where you want them, send me a note. Or a tweet.

3. You Learn New Tricks

Whether you are new to job search or an old pro, you have to be open to the new way of doing things. And, in addition to new ideas, I like to share quick tips and tricks from time to time.

4. You Build Confidence

Tim's Strategy is about the strategy and psychology of successful job search and about career and life strategy. Strategy is really important. A positive psychology (aka confidence) is critical. How? If your strategy gets you the interview but your confidence keeps you from getting the offer, you'll know. You build confidence by knowing that you are prepared for every possible scenario. And by learning how to believe in yourself.

5. You Get Entertained

I try to write the blog in a way that feels less like a self-help book and more like a fun guided tour. I'm inspired by Steve Martin, Chevy Chase and Monty Python if that helps you at all. You see, while job search can be painful, frustrating and heart-breaking it can also be a great time of reflection on what really matters in life. In between networking and interviewing, you have a unique opportunity to live, hang out with your kids and explore your passions.

6. You Avoid Simple Mistakes

We've all made them at some point. In truth, there is an etiquette in the job search world. There are ways you can strain or bruise a networking relationship or ways that you can over-communicate with a company. Regularly reading a blog can help you catch a mistake before it is made. Sound good?

7. You Meet New People

Really? Yes. But how, you say. Well, by commenting on a blog when the mood strikes. Other regular readers see your comments and can comment back to you or build on your idea. Do this long enough and you've found a friend. Someone who thinks like you do. Also, a lot of blogs have companion groups on Linkedin or Facebook. Once a member there, it is really easy to build relationships and, before you know it, you are networking.

8. You Get Encouragement

On *Tim's Strategy*, encouragement comes in two forms. First there is the traditional sort. Feels good and warms your heart. The second part can be more blunt and unsettling. That is the sort which acts as a wake up call. I've found that often the friendly encouragement will not jolt you out of a bad pattern. Here, in my experience, only a two by four (to the side of the forehead) will do. Some things cannot be said gently.

9. You Can Ask Questions

Here on the blog as well as on the Linkedin group, questions are encouraged. And most all get answered. As a later blog post, a return comment or via a personal e-mail. Unlike a big networking event or seminar where you are forced to stand up and ask in front of "everyone", on a blog you can be somewhat anonymous. And you get the benefit of the blogger's experience as well as all the other visitors whose experiences may benefit you as well.

10. You Gain Perspective

Let's face it. Some days, when looking for work, things can seem bleak. There are days when nothing happens. No one calls and no one writes. It may seem like you are the only one not getting interviews. Not true. But you'll only realize that when you hear it from other job seekers. So, to avoid living inside your own little world, open up the curtains and let the sun in. Sun = blog in case I lost you there.

Most of us writing job search blogs work very hard and sleep very little in our quest to bring you closer to your next great role. The reward is in hearing your feedback and, especially, in hearing that something we wrote or built for you helped make something happen. A new contact. A new interview. A job offer with a company you've been targeting.

In the end, your decision to become a regular blog reader on *Tim's Strategy* or on one of the many wonderful job search blogs out there is up to you. You may decide to pick and choose among ten different blogs or you may choose just one.

But, can I tell you a secret? I hope you choose mine.

6

Job Search Strategy:
Are You The Tortoise Or The Hare?

There is a job search strategy for everyone. One for those more impulsive and one for the planners of the world. The only problem is that one works better than the other.

Which one are you using? Really? Are you sure?

This is an important question. Especially for job seekers new in their search or for folks who are three months in and still trying to figure out what they are doing right and wrong.

So if you said "Hare" because you are a Type A personality and have pursued job search with reckless abandon, well, we need to talk.

If you said "Tortoise"… you, like the tortoise in the fable, will find a faster route to your next job.

Now I guess I could be done with it here by saying:

Be the tortoise.

Seems like I'd leave you hanging a bit - something I'm hesitant to do. But, really, don't you already get it? Sounds reasonable that a solid, consistent strategy will beat half-baked aggression, right?

And because it is only 11:30 PM and I don't feel good unless I write until somewhere near 2:00 AM. That gives me a good 4.5 hours of sleep before getting up and heading off to work. Some days I feel like a happy but sleepy tortoise regardless of my depth of strategy...

So since the hare and tortoise's differences are part personality type and part skill set, how does one describe those differences in the job search world?

Well, bullet points, of course! Here goes:

The Hare

• So the hare is about bursts of speed. Especially early bursts. Ones that leave everyone else feeling slow and lazy. A disconcerting feeling, to be sure. "Should I be sprinting right now?"

• The hare is also about complacency and over-confidence as early bursts may get them some early results that seem promising. But those early results risk being artificial. Supported by what can be a dangerous optimism.

• If laid off at the same time as a hare, you might witness a flurry (I almost wrote "furry") of early activity. A couple of days frantically throwing a resume together, e-mailing everyone in your network (if organized), calling 8-10 recruiters letting them know you are now available and blasting your resume to 50 or so hiring managers who have posted jobs on Monster.

• The hare is less likely to network and, unfortunately, is less likely to help others. No time, right? Gotta go!

- The hare will be less prepared to share their job objectives and would for sure not have a *Watchlyst*™ of their own.

- The hare will not have a well-thought out elevator speech. They will meander and extend 60 seconds to 5 minutes, losing everyone in a swirl of career details.

- Yes, the hare will burn out and fizzle. But only after finally realizing six months into their search that the tortoise had a suspiciously simple plan.

OK, after all that tearing down of the cute little bunny, let's see what's so great about the tortoise.

The Tortoise

- So, despite the fuddy-duddy voice used and hapless expression typically placed on a cartoon tortoise, I am here to tell you something important. The tortoise is really smart. One might say intelligent. Especially in job search.

- The intelligence comes as the knowledge of what to do, how to plan it and when to expend the energy to execute it. You see, the tortoise is all about efficiency. While the hare is racing around in impressive circles, the tortoise is preparing for a short, uneventful walk across the circle's diameter.

- The tortoise knows that preparation is key. That there is wasted effort in racing out the door before you are ready with your professional one sheet, business cards, and a really good sense of your job objectives. All those people that you meet (as the hare) will struggle in trying to help you if you can't tell them who you are, what makes you different and what, specifically, you are looking for in your next role.

- The tortoise is going to stop along the way and help someone by the side of the road. Even if it slows their speed to the finish line. They do this with the knowledge that 1 year or 5 years down the road, the situation may repeat. That network, nourished, will be needed once again!

- The tortoise also plays the part of a strategic networker on Linkedin. Looking for real connections that will drive long-term relationships.

- The tortoise has been building solid relationships with recruiters for years. They seek win-win friendships by helping recruiters find talented people in their network who might fit a search. They are rarely in a hurry when the call comes in.

- The tortoise prepares well for interviews and knows how and when to follow up without looking desperate or winded.

So, in the end, please know that job search is one part of a larger plan that requires an intelligent approach, continuous networking and the utilization of smart tools to build and maintain a successful long-term career.

And I'll tell you one other thing.

You can be part tortoise and part hare. And still be successful.

Here's when. After all your preparation and smart planning, you will get a job offer. Once you have the offer in hand and calmly walk out to the car and drive home safely…

You can race into your house to share the good news.

7

Running Through
The Pain of Job Search

I ran my first and (so far) my last marathon in 2007. While not a breathtaking course visually, the Orange County Marathon left me huffing and puffing on an unusually warm and breezy day in January.

When thinking about the marathon, it reminded me of the time that I dedicated to train for it. And the time I had later that year when I found myself looking for work. As I have shared before, while an out of work experience can be stressful and frustrating, it is also your single best opportunity to get back in shape. And it feels really good to be in shape.

So I started thinking about how I could frame some job search ideology in the context of running the marathon. Can you think of a few worthy comparisons? Well, if not, perhaps this will "jog" a few loose.

SUCCESSFUL MARATHON RUNNERS ARE:

Well trained in advance of their race day

You've heard me say it before that week one of your job search is not the best time to learn about networking. So if you have found yourself in this spot, you'll have to make do. If you are working and haven't started, well, get started. Networking is the single biggest skill you need to succeed in today's job market. And, while a good personality helps, don't plan on just winging it.

Prepared for the worst

Your job search can end happily in four to six weeks but it can also continue for six, nine or twelve months. Sometimes longer depending on the market, your industry experience and your ability to stand out in an interview process. If you plan for four to six weeks and get six months, what happens to your psychology (confidence) during weeks eight to ten? It starts to get a bit shaky, right? Now, I am not saying assume the worst. Just be ready for it. Mentally. And, for sure, financially.

Constantly looking for training partners

It may seem like it, but job search is not a solo sport. Those who choose to go it alone will find life a bit troubling. Without a community around you for support, you will struggle. Sorry if that sounds harsh. There are so many great things to be shared during this time in life - in addition to your learnings and experiences with other job seekers. Sharing job leads with others (even those in your same profession) builds good rapport and, I believe, good karma with the job search community. So, look for friends. Not as a crutch or as a social party friend. But as a partner in job search success.

Well equipped with the latest tools

Runners have all sorts of cool new gadgets and rarely will you see someone still training in Dolphin shorts. So why allow your job search to fall victim to the status quo? Old tools are for old job search strategies. Ones that are not effective in today's competitive job market. Linkedin, Twitter to name a few have to be on your list. Use Indeed for effective job leads. Don't be the one afraid to try new things. Because companies are finding their new employees with these new tools. If you're not there, you're not there.

Unwilling to give up
There are days, to be sure, that job search feels like a losing battle. No leads. No call backs. No love. If those stretch into weeks - and they can - you need to remember that you have a strategy. You are networking for a reason. You are, hopefully, acting on every opportunity to meet new people, sharing your job objectives and offering to help them in return. Or, even better, in advance. Successes will come and go. You only need one lead to turn into a job - not all of them.

Looking for new ideas
One of the things I have said about *Tim's Strategy* is that it would be about ideas. So, I offer you the blog as a relatively regular stream of ideas to help you succeed in job search. There are many other good sources. Resume writers, career coaches and recruiters all can be great sources of information.

Supportive of other racers in your group
Have you joined any networking groups in your community? Any groups on Linkedin? No? Really? If not, get started on this today. If you need help here, drop me a note and I will get you started. It is that important. In addition to offering job leads, you can share your tricks of the trade or just a shoulder to lean on. Yes, even us tough job seekers need a little warm cocoa from time to time. Want to join my group on Linkedin? The process is painfully simple. Join the group and tell 'em Tim sent you.

Confident and ready to take off on their own

So remember up above when I said that job search was not a solo effort? Well, there is a time in job search when you need to let go. When you have found that great job. The one that matches your job objectives with a culture that screams your personality and work style. And when you are ready to leave the search community and head back into the world of the working. And, believe me, there are some that cling to the freedom of job search. You also need to be confident to run when the opportunity shows itself. Without looking back as you set a pace faster than those behind you. Especially if their pace has you feeling lazy and complacent. That happens too.

8

I Can't Be Out Of Leads...
I Still Have Resumes Left!

Do you have a job search strategy? Are you sure?

Ever heard this one before?

"I can't be out of leads... I still have resumes left!"

Probably not. But if you are a recruiter or a hiring manager/HR person receiving piles of resumes, it may feel like it some days.

Of course this headline is stolen from the old joke about a false relationship between checks in your checkbook and money in the bank. But I think the concept works here. In a different way.

Here it says that job seekers mistake the ability to do something with the value in doing something. Precisely, I'm trying to help you avoid wasting your time and the time of the hiring community.

The direct advice?

Don't do things just because you can. Do them because they are part of a strong and well-planned job search strategy.
This advice has relevance in a number of places within job search. The basic point? Have a purpose for everything you do. Here are a few examples where you can be more purposeful in your decision-making during job search:

Applying For Jobs

How do you decide what jobs to apply for? Referral from a friend? New alert from Monster.com? There will always be temptations due to the nature of being in transition. Most of us in transition want to stop looking and find a job (I say most as some really love being out and free!). And anything that looks kind of close gets our heart palpitating.

There will always be a temptation to throw your resume at every position that:
1. includes your function (marketing)
2. falls in your industry (health care)
3. is at your level (director)

Why? Well, why not, right? What is hurt by you throwing your hat in the ring? One extra resume can't really overburden the system! Well, that's not the point. It's you wasting time.

Sending Resumes To Companies When No Job Exists

Generally this falls under the category of don't do it. Again, you might say, "why not?". And again I will say: why waste your time? The odds that someone in HR will open your resume, see your experience and say "Hey, we need to create a job for this person" are pretty small. You should be networking with others to find jobs that exist first.

Now, can you build relationships in target companies in advance of a job being available? Yes. And I think this makes sense. Because at that same time you can be asking for names of other companies or other contacts where there may be some jobs opening up. So, the distinction is in the method. If part of your job search strategy is to network your way into your top 5 target companies, do it in person. Sending a blind resume or including that company as part of a mass mailing campaign is a waste of time. My opinion.

Going To Group Networking Events

Again, it's decision time. There are a lot of events out there now for job seekers and serial networkers. But they are not all worth attending. If you think that you are better out every night networking than at home with family or friends, you are wrong. Networking events can be fantastic. They can also be a great time waster. Include the use of networking events as a integral part of your job search strategy and then stick to that strategy.

Agreeing To Individual Networking Meetings

As you get into your search, especially if you become a person to know, others will want to meet with you. You will also likely have a list of people that you'd like to meet. Folks who have connections in your industry, are currently working in your industry or have some other influence that you find valuable. While these one-on-one meetings can be valuable, they can also become a burden if unproductive. My thoughts here:

1. Each should have a purpose - this is not social time
2. Keep them under an hour - 30 minutes is a good target
3. Share specific job objectives - via your *SoloSheet*™ or *FlashCard*™
4. Ask how you can help and actually do it
5. Say thank you and follow-up at least once

So the message today is: Have a purpose. Do things because they are smart and efficient. Because they are a part of a larger, well planned strategy.

Now, I'm not saying there isn't room for adjustment along the way. Did I ever pursue a long shot during job search? Of course. None of us will do this perfect!

But plan the right effort. Instead of letting impulse drive your activity.

And. If you have resumes left at the end of the day... save them for tomorrow.

9

On The Job Hunt?
What's Your Angle?

A couple of weeks ago I re-learned something about life that makes for a good living analogy in job search.

It happened one afternoon as I was doing an errand at a local business office here in Mission Viejo. It started innocently enough.

I get out of the car and circle the back end of the Jeep to head up the parking lot toward a main door. Once in view of the rest of the parking lot, I notice another person apparently heading to the same building entrance. And he's walking about my same speed.

Wanting to avoid an awkward meeting at the door, I begin to pick up the pace. And, once there, I can choose whether my speed was enough to get in quickly or whether it would be easier to wait a few moments to hold the door. Does this sound anti-social? I guess it does. But it is a part of our culture so I try to have fun with it.

Am I the only one who thinks about this stuff?

Of course, the other option was to slow down and let him get there first. There, now he has the moral dilemma! But I decided I wanted to beat him there. I was in a bit of a hurry having a few more errands to run that afternoon.

Well, as I picked up the pace, I noticed that it wasn't helping. Despite a spring in my step, it appeared that all was lost. We shared a few respectful glances as we got closer and I, in respect for his apparent victory, slowed my pace and let him reach the door with a healthy gap between his and my arrival.

And, you know what? He didn't hold the door and he didn't say hello.

So what did I learn here?

He had a better angle.

And, as a result, required less effort to achieve his desired result.

And there are a lot of other examples in life where a better angle or a better approach wins the day. Think about a defensive back in football trying to run down a wide receiver streaking down the sideline. Or a center fielder in baseball running to catch up to a screaming line drive in the gap.

In the end, a better angle beats extra effort if all things are equal. And in job search, there are many equalizing factors. So it makes sense that the right angle helps when on the job hunt.

Since the origins and many of the tools created for Tim's Strategy are focused on smart, efficient activity, your angle in job search seems to be a highly relevant and practical discussion.

But, what are some examples of a better angle or advantage?

1. Your Job Search Strategy
A few weeks ago I asked the question: Are You The Tortoise Or The Hare? If you read this post, ask the question and answer it honestly, you will have a sense of the angle(s) you have used up to this point.

Have you been smart or just aggressive? Your speed may have beat the other guy to the door but were you prepared to succeed upon arrival at the hiring office?

2. Productive Networking

But, perhaps the best example is networking. Say, for example that a new job just popped up on the radar screen. A great fit with your job objectives? Great! Now, how many others in this market have the same idea? Now you and a few hundred others have sent highly polished cover letters and resumes to the hiring manager. A few have sent theirs via Fed Ex hoping to capture the eye of an HR manager. One person even tried a personal note to the CEO to see if the highest exec might be so compelled to make mention of you to the hiring manager.

What's your angle? And is it the best, most effective one? Does it include the use of your network or the network of those connected with you on Linkedin? Do you think that a referral to the hiring manager from a respected third party beats a FedEx or a CEO letter? Of course it does. Like a full house over two pair…

A word of warning, though. Don't tap your network hard for a job in which you are not qualified. Once a good hiring manager sees a lack of fit, your resume will find the trash can and your network will hear that their effort was wasted. Not good.

Now, of course, we're talking about getting a phone or first round interview. Your ability to succeed in that first interaction relies upon a different angle.

3. Vetting and Preparation

Once noticed and guided into an interview position through a smart initial approach, your job is to now make a connection with the company and show them how you, uniquely, are the right person for the job. One of the ways to do that is through vetting and researching the company and its people. And through this process and the first interview, you may find out that you don't want to work for this company. And that is not a bad thing to learn!

Vetting is a process designed to learn about and potentially weed out certain aspects of an opportunity. Also your overall preparation is key in being in a position to succeed as a candidate. If you haven't already seen it, check out my Sip™ tool. It is a free download from the *Tim's Strategy* website.

Of course there are many other examples of smart and efficient efforts in job search. You can check the archives at Tim's Strategy for other articles. I hope a number of them give you a few new ideas to help you arrive at a new job with confidence and style.

So, do yourself a favor. Be smart, have a strategy and identify the angles that will help you work productively. Leaving time during job search to pursue a few passions and spend high quality time with your family.

And if you see someone else racing toward the door... smile, wave and enjoy the walk. On the days when you get there first, hold open the door. You may make a new contact.

10

How To Measure The Success Of Your Job Search

A friend and colleague from a prior company e-mailed me today and gave me some much appreciated feedback on the blog. It is incredibly helpful to hear feedback from readers. If you have feedback on the blog, my writing style, my perspective or have ideas of topics you'd like to have me discuss, please send me a note.

After writing many posts to the blog, you'll have to forgive me for becoming a little self insulated. You can lose perspective. You are so busy "doing" that you forget to analyze results and, as necessary, make adjustments.

Reminds me a bit of how I felt some days last year during my own job search.

So, how do you measure the success of your search? A few things that strike me based on my own search process as well as discussions with fellow job seekers along the way:

1. Do you have an actionable strategy?
In my opinion, job search success comes when hard work and preparation meet up with good timing. If you are without a strategy, you will likely be "finding acorns" by accident and in ways that deliver a result but not a good one. My advice? Set specific goals for the

week that include phone calls, networking events, networking calls or coffees, etc.

2. Are you taking smart action, each and every day, to move your search process forward?

While I have said before that you can't search for a job 12 hours a day and 7 days a week, you need to be proactive. If you find yourself sitting in front of your computer waiting for e-mail alerts to arrive or scanning and re-scanning job search sites with different keywords, you are not working smart.

3. Are you getting your phone calls returned?

This is a highly measurable and important metric. The reality of this metric is important though. In my experience, a really good result is 3-4 people out of 10. A pretty good batting average in baseball, but a very frustrating result if you act diligently, put out a bunch of well thought out communications and get very little back to show for it. This includes calls into recruiters, networked hiring managers, employed people who work at a target company. If you are getting no calls back - NONE - you are either reaching too high (wrong level in a company) or too far (reaching out to people that are too distant from you relationally). If you are getting 2/10 that's not bad, but ask yourself why those two called back and see if you can, on your next round of calls, target folks that may have a better reason/motivation to help you out.

4. Are you getting recruiter calls?

Here I am not talking about while you are working - those are easy to get (everyone likes to call people who are employed, right?). I'm talking about calls specifically seeking your interest in an open search while you are unemployed. So, if you are getting these calls, what does it mean? It means a couple of things. First, people are networking for you and sharing your name with recruiters. They do this because they are aware of your availability, but more importantly, they are willing to share your name because they believe in you. Your recruiter calls are a measuring tool not only of a successful search effort but also a measurement of how well you have nurtured and respected your network.

5. Are you someone people seem to want to talk with?

If you go to a typical networking event where everyone gives their elevator speech*, there is always a period of informal networking at the end. Pay attention and you'll notice 7-8 smalls groups of 2-3 people forming. At the center of each group is one of four people. They are: the event organizer, the speaker, an employed networker who decided to show up and the 4 or 5 people who had really interesting things to say in their elevator speech. They delivered it well, displayed a confidence and made eye contact with everyone in the room as they spoke. How was your speech? Would you have approached yourself after your speech? Without a dynamic elevator speech, you will join the rest of the crowd waiting in line to network with one of the four folks mentioned above (a hard start to separate yourself).

*(an elevator speech is a 30-60 second presentation that includes a summary of your work experience, your target industry, target geography, target position, target companies and, hopefully a few memorable anecdotes about your successes - be memorable! It also never hurts to offer a few job leads to the group as it makes you valuable to others).

6. Are you getting phone interviews?

Phone interviews are a measurement of your resume's ability to quickly and substantially communicate your credibility and fit with the company's published job description. If you are getting no phone interviews, it is likely you are either applying for the wrong jobs (you are over or under qualified) or your resume is not strong enough at creating an impression. Also, a poor record on getting phone interviews can also be a reflection of an over-written, "trying too hard" cover letter. Get too cute with your cover letter and you can stand out in a negative, immature or unprofessional way - landing your resume/cover combo in the trash.

So, pay attention to the results you are getting and how people react to you. Are they introducing you to others or finding a convenient reason to move on ("Hey the buffet looks good, nice meeting you")? How do your results compare to other job seekers in your network. If everyone else is interviewing and you are busy searching for jobs on Monster, you have work to do!

Take the time once a month to stop "doing", review your results and plan for adjustments to get back on target. Good luck!

The Psychology
of Job Search

11

Landing Is For Pilots, Not Job Seekers

There's a term in the job search community for when you find a job. You "land" a new job and you send out a "landing announcement" to your network so that everyone knows you are off the market. Sounds like a positive thing to "land", right? Of course, it is a very positive thing - don't get me wrong.

But I have a different take on it. To "land" suggests to me the end of a precarious journey, a bumpy flight on "out of work" airlines. If you take that analogy a bit further, you can envision other job seekers on the flight with you and others on planes that left Chicago a few hours later who will eventually land. Still others did not impress in their last interview and were bumped from their flight, forced to wait for the first flight in the morning. Remember all the white knuckled passengers on your last flight?

If you have a solid job search strategy, however, the flight does not have to be bumpy. You will not have to wait in line at the gate hoping you get on the flight. Instead you can rest easy in the Red Carpet Club sipping a cold beer. Having a strategy not only gives you a specific plan of attack but it also provides confidence, clarity and the opportunity to actually enjoy some time off as you look for a new role.

So I'll suggest a new term for job finders called "Arrival". Next time you find that great new job, you can say you've "arrived" as if you knew it all along. Arrival sounds like it happened under your own control - in a way that was predetermined through a intelligent approach and a efficient work ethic. Instead of landing on a 737 with 165 other passengers, you will "arrive" in a 1974 Triumph TR6, with wind whipped hair and a tan.

12

Out Of Work? Lucky You...

During my recent "out of work" experience in late 2007, I got some great advice from a helpful career coach. Based on the premise that you can't possibly look for work 12 hours a day, there were some powerful ways, she said, to spend my transition time. In fact, this 3-6 month period may be the only significant block of free time in my entire adult life. What could I do with it?

While tempting initially to "play" and "roam", I knew I had to establish an early pattern of pro-active effort to get my search off on the right foot. So during the first 4 weeks I did all the right things. However, once I had my resume updated, search engine alerts set up, my recruiters contacted, my other micro networks alerted and had planned a series of networking events, I allowed myself a chance to relax. Now relaxing is a hard mind-set to justify. You have to be careful that in your own mind, the minds of hiring managers/recruiters and in the minds of key people in your network that your "search ethic" is strong. They need to know that if they recommend you for a job you will knock 'em dead and not show a lack of interest.

You see, there are folks - I've met a few - who did not engage. They did not have a sense of urgency about their job search. They got stuck in a mode of enjoyment. Watching TV, shopping on-line, grabbing a few beers at lunch, playing golf/tennis or whatever thing they so missed doing from college. Call it denial, being irresponsible or maybe just being lost (defined as not really knowing what they want to do in life), these people need what an old boss of mine used to call a "two by four to the head". Without a balance between relax/enjoy and purposeful action, there will be difficulty ahead.

So, assuming you have a strategy for your search and you have implemented the early tactics... lucky you. You have time to re-charge your batteries and, perhaps more importantly, the batteries of those around you.

Here are a few ideas for you:
1. Walk or drive your kids to school
2. Coach your daughter's soccer team
3. Volunteer at church
4. Take a drive up the coast to visit family
5. Take a class at the local university
6. Give your dog a bath
7. Start a blog
8. Re-assess your priorities in life
9. Create a short term and long-term financial plan
10. Paint your house
11. Transfer VHS family movies to DVD
12. Take to your spouse or significant other to brunch
13. Pull the old guitar out of the attic and serenade someone
14. Research your family tree
15. Organize a family reunion
16. Organize your home filing system

17. Create an estate plan
18. Pursue an entrepreneurial dream
19. Locate an old family friend and write him or her a letter (on paper with a pen)
20. Write a poem
21. Go to the gym (everyday)
22. Cook healthy dinners
23. Go to a museum
24. Re-negotiate your home, life and auto insurance rates
25. Start a family Yahoo! Group

So, take advantage of this time. It may be your only or one of a very few open doors to really connecting to the world around you. Because, if you are like me, work can become all encompassing if you let it.

I found new parts of myself during my transition. I struck a balance between search and surrender because I listened to smart people around me. I had a strategy that forced early discipline and allowed some well deserved relaxation along the way.

Lucky me.

13

The Psychology Of Job Search

In 2007, I found myself officially out of work and "in between" for the first time in 17 years. Five companies and multiple divisions of each but never on the street corner. Your first experience is part fear and part fantasy - the degree to which you sway is based, I think, on what you bring to the situation and what's happening in the job market at the time you become available.

So, I'm suggesting that at least some of the mental game can be controlled through the way you approach your search process. You will also be influenced by the way you were released back into the job market, right? Being fired vs. being laid off are two very different jumping off points. Similarly, leaving on your own because you hate your job is very different from leaving on your own to simply find a new industry. If you can be conscious of your individual situation, you can remain aware of the baggage you bring into your search process and into each interaction you will have along the way.

For example, if you were laid off or fired you are more likely to carry some resentment with you into your first interview or recruiter discussion. You are more likely to bring up negatives when explaining how you find yourself unemployed. If you left on your own accord, however, you may carry a more laissez-faire approach to your process, especially early on. In this scenario, perhaps your sense of urgency to find a job is reduced and it is obvious and potentially damaging to your success.

How about if you have been out of work for a number of months and have no really good prospects? Would you start acting unprofessionally out of desperation?

To be successful in the psychology of job search you need to have two key things:

1. A solid and proactive job search strategy
2. A clear and confident perspective on your situation

So, if you use only these two "success factors" - clearly there are many more - how well prepared are you to find a job?

Here are a few scenarios:

Without a Strategy
Your "hard work" and correct mental framework will likely, over time, shift to the negative. As you move forward without a strategy (hoping to find something), your lack of structure will result in fewer interviews and more wasted effort. Which, in turn, will have you less confident and questioning your ability to find a job.

Without a Clear Perspective
Even if you have a strong job search strategy, any baggage you bring to your interviews, networking events or recruiter conversations can sabotage all of your hard work and preparation. Worse still, a bad discussion can cause repercussions in your larger network. Yes, people talk.

No Strategy and No Clear Perspective

This is a formula for a minimum 12 month search, often resulting in a poor choice (i.e. jumping at a bad offer) that can dump you right back in the market.

So, how do you clear your head? If you were fired or laid off, don't you have a right to be angry and bitter? Perhaps you do, but before you start your active search you need to find a way to make peace with it. If you need to get it off your chest, go buy a punching bag. If you need healing (a common need after a harsh departure), there are a number of ways to find it including some time away or a few sessions with a well regarded career coach.

How did you get your perspective back?

14

Job Search...
Like An Out Of Body Experience

I was thinking the other day about how sometimes during job search it is easy to lose perspective. That if you try to go it alone without strong, helpful people around you, the search process can start to feel a bit lonely.

Then I thought while it is nice to have people around to guide you, wouldn't it even be better to guide yourself? To, in fact, watch yourself as you interview, network, meet with recruiters and introduce your job search situation to friends and neighbors. How do you think you'd look and sound?

I'll call this your "out of job experience".

I call it this because you get a unique look at yourself at a time when you are a little less confident, a little more tentative, a little less smooth. For some reason, being out of work changes you. Why is it that after let's say 20 years of work with promotions and raises along the way that a silly (and often random) thing like a layoff should change you? Can one decision by your boss or a CEO really affect 20 years of confidence building?

Yep.

If you could sit on the same side of the desk as the interviewer and receive your own words and non-verbal cues, what could you learn from it? Could you use this data to adapt and improve your next opportunity or is the laid off or unemployed "Joe" a truly different "Joe" when employed?

And then I thought:

What factors help me to be most like my 100% confident employed self?

So in the "most like" category I put "time to search", "preparation" and "the right strategy".

Time to Search
If you have time on your side, you can actually enjoy the process of looking for your next challenge. You can interview a lot, be a little picky, challenge your interviewers and pursue other interests. What does this do? It gives you confidence internally and it shows to others - important!

Preparation
Maintain your network and keep your paperwork up to date. Be well prepared for every interaction (interview, networking events, recruiter calls, etc). Don't waste people's time.

Have the Right Strategy
This is probably the most important contributor to confidence in my opinion. If you know that the networking, communication and job targeting plan you are executing is right, you are free to be bold, forthright and memorable to the market. Knowing that you have a great plan allows you to walk over small obstacles that trip up others.

Since most of us will never have a real "out of body experience", we'll just have to visualize our own rewards. All the stories I've read lead folks up, away, toward the light and back again. Sounds a bit trite, but if you can poke your head into the light, perhaps you'll come away with a few inspired ways to remain your unflappable self.

15

The Worst Days
During Job Search...

In my experience, the worst days during job search are those when nothing happens. No calls come in, no e-mails arrive, you have no events or coffees scheduled, etc.

During my job search last year, I preferred a decision or any kind of communication (even if negative) to the emptiness of a quiet day. I remember vividly a day when I came out of a networking meeting with no expectations, checked my voicemail and found three messages. Two of the three were negative but all three cleared up long lingering opportunities that had been nagging me. Despite the bad results, I was thrilled to have closure on those opportunities as it forced me to re-focus on the remaining opportunities and to kick-start a new effort.

Is this just me? I really don't like ambiguity when it comes to job search. If you love me, let me know. If not, let me go.

I had one experience during the last search where I was rushed through the process at one of my target companies, met twice with the CEO (I was even called back twice the same day). These guys loved me and wanted to move fast, right? Not so much, it turns out. After 8 interviews over three days, someone threw cold water on the fire and let it smolder for almost 8 weeks. You really have to manage expectations, right?

Question: So, how do you manage your job search to create, build and keep your momentum?

Answer: You need to drive constant activity.

This means:
1. Regular communications with your network (i.e. a quick update to let them know you are still out there).
2. Constant (but efficient) use of the web to see what's out there and, as appropriate, applying for relevant roles.
3. Creating new networking relationships through current network extensions. Ask a person in your network: who else should I be talking to?.
4. Attending networking events and walking away with no less than 5 solid new contacts.
5. Looking for ways to help people in your network. This can include helping a fellow job seeker as well as helping a recruiter find a candidate for a role that isn't quite right for you.
6. Expanding your micro network usage by identifying yet untapped groups of people who have a reason to want to help you.
7. Finding friendly but clear ways to insert your "looking for work" status to friends, neighbors and others.
8. Using your spouse or significant other as an evangelist for your search.
9. Building a clear and specific list of target companies. How can people help you if they don't know what you want?

10. Maintaining a nice set of personal, at the ready, marketing materials. Business cards, resume, one pager, elevator speech. You never know when a chance to impress will strike.

At the end of the day, if you are sitting at your computer waiting for something to happen, it won't. Results come as a result of your activity-driving efforts - not because you are a deserving, well-liked person.

The other thing to remember is that a good response rate to outbound e-mails and phone calls is about 20 percent. While you need to be careful not to burn out your network, the worse sin is in being passive or too cautious.

As a final note, be memorable and remember to thank everyone who helps you (even in the smallest ways). From my own experience in trying to help job seekers, I can tell you the fastest way to burn out, flame out or discourage those who can help you is to forget to say "thanks".

16

How Irrational Fears Prevent You From Maximizing Job Search Potential.

Sick to your stomach. Shaky. Perspiring. On edge. Heavy breathing. Or no breathing at all. Everyone reacts to fear differently. What are the outward signs that something has you afraid?

I was on a few planes this weekend and was reminded yet again of the fear people have of flying. You can see it in their eyes, in their posture and in their hands (as they squeeze the daylights out of their partner's hand). They are glancing nervously out the window looking for signs of damage and they are acutely aware of the actions of flight attendants.

As irrational as it seems, air travel scares the daylights out of some people. After all, it is incredibly safe to travel by plane. Safer than driving a car, right?

But the power of experience and suggestion is very real. What we have seen, heard or experienced is much easier to re-play in our minds than the rational reasoning of another person. When you are traveling on a plane, there are plenty of tangible symptoms that something may be wrong. Here are a few examples of things that trigger your fear of flying:

- Bumps, dips, drops, updrafts, and shakes are all very normal during plane flight. But if you are looking for them as signs of trouble, they begin to add up. Each one tightens the rope around your fists.

- There are sounds that cause concern as well. Sounds like an engine is shutting down, the clunk of the landing gear (up and down), and the noise of sudden acceleration.

- Smells. Oh yes, this is a big one. The really bad smell of the circulation system, things that smell like smoke or burning rubber. And let's not forget the coffee.

- Then there are the visual cues. Condensation on the inside of the plane. Ever been dripped on? Oil leaking on the wing. A flight attendant walking a bit too quickly down the aisle or speaking in strange code to their partner at the back of the plane.

- The time factor. Wasn't the pilot supposed to give us an update 20 minutes ago? What's happening up there? How long have we been circling?

So if this is you on a plane, know that there are others on the same plane that are completely oblivious to the threat of death and destruction that is so obvious to you. While you are eyeing the fasten seat belt light, they are finishing their second bag of peanuts, chatting away with a seat-mate and looking for another drink.

How could this be? Are they blind, deaf and dumb?

Well, rational or irrational, it is a form of hypersensitivity that can hit you on a plane, on a camp out or in, yes, a job search.

The key in job search, I think, is separating real issues from irrational ones. Real issues can be tackled. Irrational ones can derail you unnecessarily.

So here are a few examples of real issues that you must attack head on:

1. Your resume is not attracting the attention of recruiters, HR or hiring managers.
2. Your cover letter positions you in an unflattering way.
3. You interview poorly.
4. You are a selfish networker.
5. You forget to say thank you.

How about the issues that are less important? The ones that are feeding irrational fears. Well, here's my short list. You may be able to add a few of your own...

It seems like everyone else is getting interviews but me.
Unless you have a real problem (see above), you are probably getting about the same number of interviews as the average job seeker. Stop focusing on "how many" and start focusing on getting the right ones. It only takes one.

It has been a week since my interview. I must have done something wrong!
Usually not the case. It may be true that you were not the best fit for that particular job. A decision that, once made, may actually be a positive for you. Maybe they saw the poor fit that you didn't! It could also be that the company has other important things to do

(like running the company). If they like you, they will call. If they don't call? Move on.

50 resumes sent out and not one phone call.

Resume blasting is a low percentage effort. It is the least effective way to make yourself known to hiring managers. If you decide to do it, manage your expectations and your reaction if it does not deliver a call.

Someone says you are "not qualified"

This will happen. But do not take it as a snub or think "I guess I'm not good enough". If you read the job description and specification, were you qualified? If not, why did you apply? Try to be objective.

Your focus on these issues will do nothing but leave you less confident, nervous and distracted. None of which will help you appear to be the right person to hire in your next interview.

So, stop paying attention to those irrational fears. If you have legitimate improvement areas, then get them fixed. If not…

Buckle up and grab a bag of peanuts. We'll have you back in the air in no time.

17

How To Avoid
The Stigma Of Being Unemployed

Tonight I turn once again to a question from a member of the Tim's Strategy Linkedin Group. I am very lucky to have such great members who ask intelligent questions and actively work to help their fellow group members.

The word of interest above is, of course, STIGMA.

So, I often like to start with a definition from dictionary.com. To understand where a word came from and how it is being used in this context.

The modern definition is:
"A mark of disgrace or infamy; a stain or reproach, as on one's reputation".

The archaic or ancient definition:
"A mark made by a branding iron on the skin of a criminal or slave.

Now that we have the definitions out of the way, let me just say I think this word feels really inappropriate in the context of job search. I know people can feel a bit tarnished after a lay-off.

But why?

Part of it has to do with an expectation you will have a job (everyone does, right?). If you don't or if it takes a little longer to find one, what does that make you?

Lazy? Undesirable? A non-contributing member of society? Hardly.

So there is a "stigma argument" here because society says that working is good and not working is bad (even if you are working your tail off to find employment).

But is the stigma more something job seekers put on themselves? Is it largely self-inflicted?

Do some people with jobs look down on those who are without jobs? Of course they do. This is a display of ignorance, however, as they likely have yet to experience an employment gap. When they do, they will experience a very teachable moment.

Others have experienced the over-zealous networker. The job seeker who is all about their own needs. If I try to help them, I may regret it. They'll squeeze me for more than I can give.

So, if my theory is correct that the stigma of being unemployed is mostly job seeker driven, then we should be entirely able to remove its influence by ourselves.

But how?

To answer the question:

Do Not Define Yourself As An Unemployed Person
You've heard me say before that a key to good networking is to tell everyone that you are looking. And through tools like the

SoloSheet™ and the *FlashCard™* you can make sure those people know your objectives so they can help you.

But, and this is important, do not start your conversations with "Hi, my name is Mike and I'm in transition". That's not interesting! Establish (or re-establish) a relationship with your network based on the larger, more interesting you. The one that loves to waterski. The one that writes screenplays. The one that is a competitive triathlete. Make me interested in you first. Then you can ask for my help.

Act Like Someone Worth Knowing

This is not a swagger or a cockiness. It is a quiet confidence that years of success in business can create. You just have to find that feeling again or at least project it to the crowd when attending a networking event. People want to meet and help people who believe in themselves. If you are really having a tough day and have lost some confidence, find it before you enter the room.

Ask Appropriately

Let your relationship drive the size of your request. If you've just met, be careful. You have little political capital to spend and, in fact, may be on thin ice to ask for anything. If you have a 10 year relationship of positive give and take, well, feel free to ask for what you need. As I mentioned above, those who ask for the world in a new networking relationship can spoil the soup.

Be Ready To Help Others

When you dedicate a portion of your job search to helping others, you take the focus off of your plight for a few hours a day. The less time you worry about your situation, the less you will FEEL like a victim of the lay-off or whatever event got you out looking for a new role. And, using a tool like the *Watchlyst™* you all of a sudden become a wanted commodity. You are adding value to the community of job seekers out there. So, I believe the stigma is yours to remove. In fact, it's your choice as to whether it can attach itself to you in the first place. Agree?

18

The Danger of Being
an Optimist in Job Search

In 1969, a movie was released called "Paint Your Wagon". It starred Clint Eastwood, Lee Marvin and Jean Seberg. The movie is a classic but the theme song has me troubled.

How can I be troubled by a song in an old western? You had to ask. Because I started singing it in my head the other night and it hasn't left me since.

So I decided to write about it tonight... when I should probably be sleeping.

Anyway, the chorus of the theme song goes like this:

"Where am I going, I don't know.
When will I get there, I ain't certain.
All I know is I am on my way!"

But I'll tell you the real reason it troubled me. Because it seems to be a song or a message floating through the minds of a lot of job seekers. Especially folks who are early in their search or are searching for the first time in their career.

The positive side of this chorus is that it represents an eternal optimism. An impulsive and uplifting attitude of "This shouldn't be too hard!". A sense that all you need to do is hop on the horse and head out.

Now before I begin the process of tearing down a beautiful thing like optimism, please know that I am a positive and "can-do" person. Really. But when optimism gets in the way of productive fear, I get a bit concerned.

So, what is productive fear? Productive fear is that sense of urgency you feel when you sense that perhaps you are behind or unprepared for something coming up in life that is really important to you. It is the realization that you have not taken the steps necessary to deliver your best work.

So, I dare say, optimism is the enemy of successful job search.

And productive fear drives action. Action to create a strong job search strategy. And action to seek out intelligent tools to help you succeed.

Optimism causes a number of critical mistakes and, made early on, they can severely hamper your effort.

How?

1. Assuming that your search will take 6-8 weeks.
Gosh, that would be great! Does it happen? Yes. Often? No. Please do not assume that your search will be quick. After the 8 weeks are up and frustration kicks in, you will wish you had those 8 weeks back.

2. Relying on recruiters.

Recruiters are a fantastic resource and a possible source of job opportunities. But recruiters cover only about 10% of the jobs out there. Should you work to build long term relationships with recruiters? Of course! Should you expect that your next job will come through one of their searches? No. It is unlikely and represents a false sense of security.

3. Believing that your current network will be enough.

None of us know enough people. If you think you know enough, you may think your work is done. Don't let your mind go there. In job search networking, breadth (the number of people you know), depth (the influence of that network) and education (the specifics job objectives you've shared) should be relied upon before hoping that your circle is already large enough.

4. Placing all of your eggs in one basket.

Sometimes in job search, an early win appears on the horizon. Boy that feels good. It reinforces all of your optimistic views. "See world! No big deal!" Within a few weeks of your being out of work, a great opportunity comes along. You are interviewed once, twice and now a third time. All looks good. You begin to get comfortable in the possibilities of a short search and potentially the idea that you can "bank" some severance pay. The problem comes when you don't get the job. Or the job gets put on hold or something else delays your passing "GO". Meanwhile you did not pursue other opportunities. You did not do any networking. Whoops.

5. Your brain writes checks that your body can't cash.

Your psychology (and that of your spouse) gets a wake up call. The shift from optimism to panic happens pretty quick. But its not abrupt or overt. It manifests as a slight trickle of sweat on the brow. But inside it can progress quickly into a feeling that can freeze you rather than motivate you. Productive fear, discussed above, requires a conscious understanding that a day will come early on when its time to get serious. Optimism can blind your ability to get the conscious signal.

So instead of optimism, here's what I'll suggest.

Starting day 1:
- *Build a rock-solid job search strategy.*
- *Create fantastic marketing materials that position you as the person who can deliver a big impact.*
- *Network like crazy and don't stop doing it. Make it a lifelong hobby.*
- *Be a confident, memorable and interesting person.*
- *Don't let one positive event slow your effort to create six more events.*

Be positive, sure. But optimism alone will only hurt you. Job search is serious business. It's competitive. And anything that suggests you can ease up on the throttle in the middle of the race, is unproductive.

I'd rather you be confident - knowing you have done everything possible to allow your hard work to intersect with good timing as soon as possible.

Are you an optimist?

19

The Power Of Music
During Job Search

I'm kind of a Buddy Holly fan. His music, like many others of his generation had a simple and pure energy. An energy that I found lacking some days during my last job search.

The idea here is that job search requires a certain confidence. A solid belief in yourself that can be lost through a series of rough spots, an extended search or simply a bad day.

And when things got tough for me, on some days, I turned to music. And I still do - on days when I feel like I need a lift. In fact, there's a certain Buddy Holly song that does it for me called "Rave On". There's also The Kinks. My favorite band of all time - and a certain song called "Better Things".

Now, do you have to be a music lover for this to work? I don't think so. But only you can tell me how it fits in your life - job search or not.

Now I can feel some of you heading toward the virtual door. Too touchy-feely? Yes, there's some of that here. But let me give you some ideas of how it can work for you.

1. Its early on in your job search and you have a ton of work to do on your resume. Work that is sometimes tedious and may feel like you are focused on very fine points. How about some music to calm you and help you stretch out the process instead pulling out your hair or turning on the TV?

2. Heading to the interview and need a confidence boost or timely distraction? How about a reminder of your glory days when you couldn't do anything wrong? Here I'm thinking Bruce Springsteen, John Mellencamp or Bryan Adams. Look for upbeat songs that get you moving and, even better, singing out loud. Another really good and more modern one is Green Day.

3. Need to bask in the glory of a great interview day? How about a loud opera with the windows down? Madame Butterfly works well. Sounds like victory.

4. Planning your future? Trying to decide on your life plan as part of a larger job search strategy? How about Vusi Mahlasela? I listened to him through the Oakland airport one day and ended up taking two laps around the departure area to get through the album. Also good here? Ben Harper.

5. Feeling a bit stressed? I like Steve Martin's "Wild and Crazy Guy" as comedy always seems to work for me on those days. Another good option is reggae. Bob Marley or Jimmy Cliff.

But, tell me. What role does music play in your life and how does that change when in stressful or provocative situations (like job search)?

While you are thinking, here are my two theories on music.

Music stirs up your blood.

When you are nervous or tense (pre-interview?), music helps get your blood flowing. It shakes loose the nerves and helps you to think. Especially if you pick the right song at the right time and at the right volume they seem to make sense.

Music has healing power.

Post-interview, when it is time to power-down, music can take you to a happy place and ease you back into the rest of your day. So you can contemplate what happened and confidently plan your next steps.

OK. Your turn. What are your favorite types of music and how do you use it to get you through all this? Drop me a note.

In the end I hope you, like Buddy Holly, will be smiling and full of energy.

20

The Benefit Of A
Quick Backward Glance

Your career. No matter how long you've been at it, your career has a memory and a history that deserves recognition. Now before that idea goes way over all of our heads, let me say it a different way. There is a benefit to looking back.

Some say "don't look back" and "the past is the past". Hogwash.

I believe there is tremendous learning to be done not only in retrospect but, more importantly, in watching how you changed as a result of each experience. As a result of each boss. As a result of each company. And as a result of each co-worker.

I have always told people that I learned something great from every boss or mentor I've had in my career. Sometimes it was learning what not to do, however. Here are some examples of both:

Thanks - I had a boss early in my career (when I was still wearing fancy suspenders) who, having noticed the commitment I was making to the company, invited me to his office and handed me $100. He wanted me to take my wife out for a nice dinner since he knew my quality time was being spent at the office. I will never forget the impact of that gesture.

Punctuality - My first sales trainer chewed me up one side and down the other when I arrived with a clean car, a perfectly organized sales book and a nice suit. Problem is I arrived on time - not 15 minutes early (his view of on-time).

Pressure - The first time I (at age 22) worked with my region manager to show him my new territory it was a cold and snowy day in Denver. He gets in my company car, puts a cup of coffee (no lid) on the dash and says "Let's go. Don't spill the coffee". I think this was his version of my walking on rice paper. Guess what? It spilled.

Common Sense - In the old days of entertainment budgets and getaway sales meetings, our region's finance guy decided to have a few extra drinks during dinner, brought an extra beer on the bus for the ride back to the hotel and proceeded to pour the beer over my head. He later was seen crawling through the hotel lobby with no shirt and no shoes. It reminded me of The Shining (Jack Nicholson).

Feedback - A prior supervisor was not good at reviews. Check that. She didn't give them. For two years. Needless to say, I was under whelmed and always vowed to make reviews an important part of the relationship with my teams.

Team - I worked for a VP/GM who created a very powerful and efficient team. We succeeded in ways that I had never seen before and we did it through teamwork. There were no sales or marketing boundaries, no arguments between quality assurance and product development. This team had a clear mission and, by the way, we spent a lot of time together having fun and winning.

So this is one way to look back. To review the people and your experiences with them. Especially those that shaped you in your young career.

So how does this relate back to job search?

Well, as I look back, I:

- *did not always make the right decisions*
- *twice lived with a horrible commute (2+ hours each way on some days)*
- *worked long hours to get projects complete only to find them delivering minimal impact*
- *accepted job offers to solve a problem vs. to complete a well thought out strategy*
- *allowed others to steer and influence my career - eventually taking a very traditional path*

Were these examples good or bad for my career and life? Not sure. Although a few of them seem very short sighted now. Regardless, each decision I made back then, along with the resulting experience, prepared me for the future. And, in their own unique way, each experience and decision make me who I am today.

The other value of looking back is to see patterns and to see (as only hindsight will allow) the logic in decisions that did not seem so logical at the time. For example, I interviewed ferociously for jobs that seemed perfect at the time. Now looking back I see the reasons why I was not hired and I realize that the company made the right decision for us both. Had I only known then!

If we could only see the patterns forming before us, we could be so much more confident and directed in our job search efforts, right?

So since we can't see forward we must use our memory of what it is like to look backward. And seeing those patterns, try to realize that actions by a recruiter, hiring manager or company that did not benefit you will likely be made reasonable and correct once the right context is added a few years down the road.

What are the practical lessons for this?

- *If you don't get a call back when you thought you would, let it go.*
- *If you were really close to getting a job offer but didn't, move on.*
- *If recruiters aren't calling you back for a job that seems perfect for you, it isn't.*

Every one of these small decisions will form into a larger pattern. Confidently approach your job search but don't fight the results. You'll likely see the wisdom someday and can begin to see your own pattern.

Young in your career? Don't worry, we've trampled a path for you.

Smart
Networking

21

11 Keys To Successful Job Search Networking

OK. I am going to cover a topic that an awful lot of people still struggle to grasp. I don't blame them, but I really want them to figure it out. It is in some ways really simple. And other ways painfully difficult.

The subject is networking. Clearly this is a topic covered by many-a-blogger so I hope this short case study knocks a hole in the wall for you and lets some light in. I'll try to keep it painless.

I had an experience a few weeks ago with someone I knew from earlier in my career. We briefly worked at the same company in the early 1990's. But we hadn't spoken since then. So why was this experience a good one and what specifically happened between us that left me with such a good impression?

1. Staci re-connected with me via Linkedin. Although we were not connected there yet, she found me and sent a personal and friendly note asking if I would meet with her. Since she sent a personal and friendly note, I am now instantly open to hear what Staci has to say. She took the time to make me feel important by spending a few extra minutes on that note.

2. We met at a coffee shop near my house. Staci could have suggested that we meet in the middle (she lived in Los Angeles and I am in Orange County). Her decision to drive to me shows a respect for my time. Let's face it, she made it really easy for me to say yes.

3. She offered to buy my cup of coffee. Not everybody does this - in fact, most don't. Those who do, again, send a clear message of appreciation. It doesn't matter if that message has a value of $2.50. It still matters. A few months ago I met with a recruiter and got some advice on the blog. While that recruiter wouldn't let me buy breakfast that day, you better believe she got a gift card from me a few days after our meeting!

4. Providing some early value is critical. Staci did this by bringing a CD filled with recruiter names and company lists that she thought I could use. I felt appreciated and thankful for the effort on her part.

5. During our meeting, I gave her everything I could including resume feedback, an introduction to the free downloads on Tim's Strategy, etc. I told her everything I knew about the market for jobs down here and finished our meeting absolutely spent. But happy that I could help and glad that we had connected.

Now it could have ended there (as most networking relationships do). But here's how Staci extended our relationship and made me want to stay involved in her search...

6. At the end of our chat, she said those magic words: "Tim, how can I help you?". I've learned to always have an answer for this one. I told her that if she knew of anyone who might be helped by the Tim's Strategy blog or website to please send a note or let me know. Simple, right?

Over the next week, Staci reinforced her interest in building a great relationship.

7. She introduced me (and *Tim's Strategy*) to two people who run an outplacement company in Los Angeles. These are great targets for my content as they are always looking for new ideas to help their job seeker clients. And I love new ideas!

In between here, I sent her leads on two great career coaches - something she mentioned during our meeting as an interest area.

8. She sent me contact information for the head of her graduate university's alumni career center. Again, a place where potentially I can gain additional exposure for Tim's Strategy.

9. She attended a networking group presentation of mine and made sure to grab me before and after to re-connect. She also sent me a note after to tell me how much she enjoyed it.

10. She commented on a blog post and offered some very relevant thoughts on the topic. As a blogger, comments are an important part of interacting with readers and they also help support better search engine results by showing the value of your blog to the community. She helped me.

11. She followed up weeks later to let me know how she was doing and very succinctly updated me on her situation. A very helpful reminder that she was still out there.

Now, every networking relationship is different. Clearly the stars aligned a bit to allow for Staci and I to meet and work well together. But you can implement a version of every one of these ideas. Yes you can.

A couple of key things to notice here:

Staci made a pretty big and broad effort to say thanks to me - before, during and after our meeting. Most important, I think, was her post-meeting effort. She went out of her way to help me. Based specifically on my answer to her question - remember those magic words? While I will remember her gracious offer to meet me near my home and buy the coffee, I will appreciate her referrals as those that added long-term value and addressed something that is really important to me. That is, the opportunity to increase awareness of this concept which I've worked so hard to create.

She maintained contact for a few weeks - cementing her search objectives in my mind. Instead of a quick thanks and monthly e-mail follow-ups, Staci delivered value in multiple steps. As a marketer, she clearly understands reach and frequency!

Staci has left me feeling like I got the better end of the deal. Why does that matter? It matters because her need is still in my head. I feel like I owe her a referral or a lead to balance out our networking relationship. Not literally, but I do want to help and she has given me 11 reasons to be looking out for her.

Last thing?

Smart networking is hard work. Because you have to prepare and execute a plan with each person. You have to know what to ask for and what to provide in return.

And you also have to know when and where to put in the bigger efforts. Had I been a junior IT professional, perhaps Staci would have focused her energies elsewhere. But I am a good contact for

Staci (as she is for me) because we are in the same industry and in the same function.

It's not always as simple as a coffee and a thank you.

But it's a start!

22

Tell Your Job Search Network What You Want

Sounds reasonable, right? "Tell your job search network what you want". Yet I can't tell you how many people don't really know or have a very difficult time getting it across. The result? A network that wants to help, but sadly, cannot.

An example: Last year I attended a structured networking event sponsored by a popular recruiting firm here in Southern California. These events put you at a table with other job seekers. The goal is to build new connections by sharing backgrounds and career objectives. The first person I was connected with was not ready to network - as evidenced by the following exchange:

ME: So, tell me about your situation and how I can help.

HIM: Well, I'm looking for something new, something more interesting. You know?

ME: What industry are you targeting?

HIM: Well, I've been in finance for the last five years and before that I was an accountant. So, something like that would be good.

ME: Do you have a geographic preference?

HIM: Not really. Wherever I can find something good.

ME: Who are your target companies?

HIM: I'm looking for something stable, companies that are strong and growing.

ME: Any job titles that would help me think of you when I hear of job openings?

HIM: Well, I'm a manager now so I would do that again. But really I'm open to anything.

This networking event was a waste of time for him as I assume all of his other conversations that night went down in flames.

This is why I push so hard for people to have a strategy! Instead of adding my "new friend" to my list of people I am looking out for as jobs pass before my eyes, I completely forgot about him. Actually I will always remember him for that conversation, but I quickly forgot his story because it was not made tangible and memorable. Honestly, if I met 10 people that night, I will be happy if I can add 2-3 people to my Watchlyst™.

It's hard to remember everyone. So… be clear, be specific, be memorable.

23

9 Ways To Bruise A Networking Relationship

In chapter 21, I shared 11 Keys To Successful Job Search Networking. You see, someone in my network knocked my socks off and, as a result, has me looking for extra ways to help.

So, as you might expect, there are those who have NOT knocked my socks off. In fact, their actions left me wanting to double knot the shoe laces. Bad people? No, not at all. Maybe lazy. Or perhaps, just perhaps, these folks had never been in a positive networking environment before. One in which people give first - not as a result of being helped in advance.

Which brings me to a point I've been wanting to make for a few weeks now. There's a term out there (now adapted for networking) which I really want to adjust. The term?

Pay It Forward

Now, you may think me a bit unfortunate for picking on a few simple and inspirational words. But these words assume one thing that I'd like to challenge.

It assumes you have to be helped before you can help others.

Not true, of course. In fact, some of the best networking happens to others before they even know what hit them. So, don't wait for inspiration. Don't wait for help. **Take action** when an idea strikes. Especially if that action is a selfless one.

So, from now on, just give.

Now back to our story... 9 Ways To Bruise A Networking Relationship.

My son plays Little League baseball and I am the classic parent volunteer. I've managed teams and have been a member of the board of directors. But probably my biggest commitment has been umpiring. One thing you need to know about this job? Little League is a place where umpire bruises are more common than base hits. Or so it seems.

Most of the bruises come from foul balls (accident), pitches glancing off the catcher's glove (accident), miscommunication (a fastball when the catcher was expecting a curve ball) and a pitch that hits nothing on the way to the plate except, at the last second, the soft underbelly of the umpire (slow/unskilled catcher). And, yes, it hurts.

Just last week, a fastball directly to the forehead got me thinking about this idea...

So in networking, as in Little League baseball, there are plenty of examples of how bruising happens. And, as I said earlier, there are fairly innocent causes for poor networking. But it doesn't matter the cause. The result is a damaged relationship and a drop off in critical networking support.

In my experience, there are three types...

(A) An accident

(B) A miscommunication

(C) A lack of skill or experience

And if you avoid these mistakes while looking for ways to emulate Staci (see the link referenced at the beginning of the chapter), you will find good things happening in your networking relationships.

9 Ways To Bruise A Networking Relationship

1. Ask for more than you deserve

So I just met you and you want what? My three best recruiters? But I hardly know you! If you ask for help that stretches beyond your relationship, you put your new networking contact at risk. If you are not sure, it's OK to ask. But don't assume.

2. Forget to follow-up

After our first meeting I send you the name of someone I know in one of your target companies. I even send your resume to that person with a light suggestion that they give you proper consideration. You do not even bother to let me know you received the e-mail. And you don't call the company contact. You have taken my time and the time of my network. Not good.

3. Disregard a reciprocal request

We are networking together as job seekers. I provide a few ideas and names of folks you should contact. I did this within a few days of our meeting. Oh, and I was hoping you could e-mail the contact information of someone in your network. You don't. You now force me to ask again. And perhaps again.

4. Forget to ask: "How can I help you"

Never assume a one-way relationship. And do not assume that your help is unwanted. Until you ask, you never know. And even if the help isn't needed now, it may be needed down the road. And your offer should stand as an ongoing one.

5. Don't say "thank you"

Say it that day. Say it each time. Say it in a follow-up e-mail. Say it with a gift card. Just say it. Gratitude feels good to the giver. It reinforces the effort and promotes more of it. And, frankly, it's not just the right thing to do... it's expected.

6. Misrepresent your relationship

So, we just met and I got your resume into a hiring manager and that, in turn, resulted in a phone interview. Great! Now what do you say when asked: "How do you know Tim?" Please be honest. If you try to create a history where one does not exist, you can create issues for both of us.

7. Over-use a contact or referral

A different example here. I give you the name of a recruiter that often has searches in your industry and at your level. I did this because I thought YOU were a good fit. Not 10 other people you know. By sending your friends the name of my recruiter contact, you could harm my relationship with them as well as fill up their in box with candidates that do not fit.

8. Make a new networking contact work too hard

Remember how Staci made it so easy for me to meet with her? She made the drive. She let me pick the time based on my schedule. So the opposite looks like this: You are requesting a meeting and ask me to drive 20 minutes. On a day that isn't ideal for me. I may go but I won't like it. And I may not be as warm and welcoming as a result. I really do want to help, but remember, if you are out of work you have time on your side. Your contact may not.

9. Assume people will help you because you need it

The reality is that there are hundreds of people to help and not enough folks willing to do it. So, how do the people with the will and time to help decide who to spend time with? They listen to the voices of those who are asking. They see it in their eyes. They look for an authentic glimmer that says: I have a need right now. I'm open to your ideas as to how I can network into a new opportunity. Oh, and I'm willing to give back.

So, "why 9?" You ask.

Well, I penalized this list by 2 (from the "11 keys") due to its focus on the negative aspects. I also wanted you to tell me your #10. What have you seen out there? What did I miss and how can your experience help one of your fellow readers?

So, tell us. But be careful. **Some of us bruise easily.**

24

Quick Tip - Network With Employed People

During job search you meet a lot of people, some who will become lifelong friends and others who will simply be another person in your network. But during job search, who should you be talking to? Fellow job seekers are easy to meet. They need help, you need help. It is a natural partnership assuming they are not the defensive or greedy type, hoarding all of the good job leads.

Anyway, while networking with fellow job seekers is largely comfortable and low pressure, I recommend at least half of your networking be done with employed people. Why?

First, they have jobs and people with jobs often have more credibility to recommend you than those who do not.

Second, it opens you up to a whole new group of people who can tell you about the most important jobs there are - real ones at real companies. Remember the fact that only 10% of jobs go through recruiters?

Q: Where do you find out about the 90%?

A: From the people who work at the hiring companies.

It's still networking. Just networking with a different crowd and with a different purpose.

25

Networking Tip - Always Pay For Lunch

If you are out right now looking for a job and are tapping into your network, please make sure that your network is appreciated. This quick tip is about saying thank you, in a proper way, each and every time you tap your network.

So, if you request a lunch meeting or a coffee meeting with someone in your network, you need to pay for it. Sound fair? What if you are many months into your search and dollars are short? You should still offer to pay for lunch.

Why? Because your network, unless we are talking your family or close friends, is not a free resource. It needs to be respected, nurtured, and appreciated.

Also, it is in your best interest. If you have a nice lunch with a recruiter, for example, and take 45 minutes of their time, get free advice and you don't offer to pay for the meal, how do you think you will be remembered? "The interesting candidate who didn't respect my time".

Harsh, but true.

26

The #1 Networking Tool During Hard Times

I'll be honest. I've been struggling.

I'm struggling to keep up with the requests of recruiters and job seekers who are networking with me to either find appropriate jobs or find appropriate candidates for current jobs.

I'm not saying that I am popular in this sense. And it's not that the number of requests is in the hundreds. I know that recruiters and career coaches are being overwhelmed with requests as the economy hands out more layoff notices each week. I am only getting my share of requests because I have actively helped people in the past.

Here's my problem. I need a simple system to connect the needs and desires of job seekers with the specs and requirements of recruiter or other networked jobs.

I belong to a number of job networks that provide daily e-mails of new jobs - many of them not recruiter driven. Often these are the ones you don't hear about on Monster, Career Builder or Indeed. Part of the problem is that the information comes in from multiple sources (phone, e-mail, conversation, etc) and my ability to cross-reference everything is limited.

Here's a scenario: I see anywhere from 15-30 new jobs a day on these networks for positions in Southern California. Each nicely spells out the job requirements, location, title, industry of the position. I then have to dig back through all of the information, e-mails, resumes, notes to find the job seekers who asked for my help.

It is painful.

In the end, sometimes I can't do it. We're all busy, right?

So you've probably guessed that the #1 networking tool during hard times is helping friends, family, former co-workers and other worthy folks find their next job. Whether you are employed or working at the time, it simply does not matter.

It also does not matter whether you are successful in this endeavor. Your effort will be remembered and the value to you is two-fold. First, you get to help someone solve a significant problem. Second, this person, once re-employed, will do anything to help you in the future. You become a person of interest, not just someone they met while out of work. Of course, not everyone will respond this way – some still don't get it – but the smart ones will understand that returning favors makes sense.

Also, as Bill Murray's character in Caddy Shack famously said: *"Oh, uh, there won't be any money, but when you die, on your deathbed, you will receive total consciousness".*

So, how did I solve this problem? A simple spreadsheet. I call my solution the *Watchlyst*™

How it works:

1. Simply enter the information for each of your contacts that are looking, print it out and keep it in your briefcase or next to your computer.

2. Every time a job comes across your e-mail, take a quick look at your *Watchlyst*™ and quickly compare for a match. If you get one, send a quick e-mail with a link to the job and a helpful "Good luck!".

3. When recruiters call, you can quickly say, yes, I know someone or no, no one in my network fits that description. Recruiters will appreciate a quick answer.

4. As new friends ask for your support, make sure they help you fill in every box on this form. Any unfilled box means you are one key piece of information short in helping them find their next role.

If you like this simple tool, send it on to a friend. But whether you use this tool or simply tap your photographic memory (my oldest son is that way, too), please take the time to network by helping others.

For those of you technically minded folks, I am also thinking about a piece of software that will do the linking for you, creating an auto-email. Even easier!

So, help a friend. There will be plenty of thanks to go around.

27

Networking Events.
Should I Stay Or Should I Go?

I go through this little dance in my head sometimes. And I'm not a very good dancer.

The dance involves my re-thinking a prior decision. I am, like many of you, busier than ever these days. More careful about the decisions I make. Wanting to be sure that I am placing myself in the right places and situations to get the most out of life.

This particular dance has to do with networking events. Both in terms of the decision to go to and when to leave the event.

Now why, you might ask, would I ever hesitate? Well, first as I mentioned above, we all get busy. We can't network every night of the week without sacrificing time at home with family, exercise, etc. Sometimes you just need a night at home, right?

There's also the issue of efficiency. Some networking events are better than others. Some are more structured giving the attendee a guaranteed chance to meet others in their industry or even a chance to meet with recruiters or hiring managers. Others, unfortunately, are so unstructured that it takes a highly proactive and outgoing person to get around the room effectively.

So, if you find yourself asking the question:

Should I stay or should I go?

Here's my take on both...

A. Should I go?

Obviously this is an individual decision that you make based on your week, your situation, the needs of your family and the perceived value of the event.

But I'll tell you that on the nights I question if I should go... and did... I am always surprised at how much value I receive. I either met a great new contact or I picked up a critical new lead or perspective.

It makes me wonder about all the events I decided to skip. What did I miss those nights? Did that decision delay my arrival at a new job? Did my decision limit my access to a great opportunity?

But I also have been to a lot of them and only by going to a wide variety was I able to decide for myself which ones to continue attending. And those that were miserable.

B. Should I stay?

So, once you get there, how do you decide when to leave? After all, it's not like a wedding reception where you can leave the second the knife cuts through the cake.

Some of the criteria I use include:

Who's there? If everyone looks familiar, you may want to head out after a quick walk around the room. Also, if all the attendees are fellow job seekers, recognize that while it is helpful to know, network with and help other job seekers, you need to be at events where working folks also hang out. After all, they are the ones who know about many of those hidden jobs, right? Also, are they at or above your level or are they all a lot younger? If a lot younger, can they help you?

How are they dressed? If too casual, this crowd may be getting too comfortable in their transition. Remember I've suggested that you take advantage of this time in your life. But do not let yourself get too lazy or too social. Go to these events with a specific purpose - not to build a social life.

Are they drinking? While there are some great events that include wine, be wary of events at or near bars. If you get there and find people heading back to the bar, you may want to find another event or head home early.

Is there structured networking? Usually structured networking makes an event better. It guarantees some sort of result for you. A new contact, a lead or a new insight as to what others are trying and what works. If no structure, consider looking for an exit unless you feel a compelling reason to stay.

Is there a speaker? If yes, it suggests a good organizer and someone who cares. Of course, there are many good events that do not have speakers, but a speaker guarantees you will get something for attending.

But first, do this. Before you actually do leave, make sure you've given the event a chance. At the point you think you should leave, give it one last try.

Because sometimes, just when you think you're done…

You meet someone who changes your situation for the better.

And that's worth going - and staying - for.

28

FlashCard.™ Introducing A New Business Card for Networking.

If you haven't been following along, much of my effort lately has been in developing tools. For you. Tools to help maximize your effort during job search. And the downloads are all free.

OK, I guess they are not totally free. If you would, I'd love to count you as a regular blog reader. And I'd love it if you would tell your friends about the blog and the tools. Mostly free, I guess.

This most recent series of tools has been about establishing a solid set of personal marketing materials. I call the whole set my Full Pitch™ series as I hope they help you hit the street with confidence. Confidence, a really good sense of who you are and what specific ways you can positively impact the people you'll be meeting that day.

So far, you've heard of the *SoloSheet™*. A one-sheet template that gets all of your critical information onto one, easy-to-digest page. It includes data that will help your network help you - something a resume does not accomplish.

Well, I have another FREE download to share. Like the *SoloSheet*, this download is my version of something that is not new. It is a template for a business card you can use while networking.

Now for all of you who already have a personal business card, be patient with this next paragraph. You are one step ahead.

For the rest of you who are not using business cards as part of your job search communication strategy, it's time to get started. Why? Well, it gives you a very common and socially accepted tool in business. It also helps you feel valuable and shows personal pride. OK, so it makes you feel like you are still in business. Great.

But most cards I've seen are bland and include very little information for someone to take-away from your encounter. Certainly nothing actionable.

So I created a new format that I'd like you to consider. It gets key data about you onto a very portable item. One that, once properly filled out, will make for a great reminder of how someone in your network can help you.

And I came up with a name for them. Sorry, I can't help it. I'm a marketing guy.

Instead of a business card, I call it a *FlashCard*™. Why *FlashCard*, you ask? Well, simply, it allows people to remember you and, this is crucial, your specific job objectives... in a flash.

So, on the front is much of the standard info (name, e-mail, phone number) you might expect. What's been added is your positioning statement (right off your one-sheet and resume), 4-6 key strengths (to help people line you up with specifics on a job description) and your Linkedin profile (make sure that your profile is fully filled out and represents you well). Overall, the front tells people who you are and how they can get in touch with you. I also left some room at the top if you wanted to add a design element.

The back is where the *FlashCard* becomes highly actionable. While I do not recommend putting career objectives on a resume, it is crucial that your one-sheet and business card have them. These are the two key documents that you will use in networking, right? How can someone effectively help you if they forget your objectives? Be as specific as you can and you will get good leads in return. Make sure to include 5-6 target companies. Not everyone you are targeting, but ones that will help people as they see a job flying by in their in-box.

You may notice the last line on the back:

Add me to your *Watchlyst*™ at www.timsstrategy.com

Remember the watchlyt is a networking tool that helps you keep track of the job objectives of those in your network looking for a job. Me? Help other job seekers? Yes, absolutely. The *Watchlyst* gets everything on one sheet so you no longer have to shuffle through a pile of resumes to figure out who should receive that new job lead.

Your job is to get your objectives on the *Watchlyst* of as many people as you can. If successful, you will receive more qualified leads and your network will feel good that they were able to help. If you are not a *Watchlyst* user or do not see the value, you can easily take that copy off the template when you design your cards.

Here's how the template works. This is a simple Microsoft Word (.doc) template. Once downloaded, you can create your cards (front and back) pretty quickly. I did mine by purchasing an Avery product (#8877) called Clean Edge business cards. You can pick them up at any office superstore. I like this method because you can print as many as you want. If you want to change anything on the card, you can do it any time and be back on the street that same night!

Of course, you can get cards printed many ways.

If you need it, the template is a free download from the website... and, good luck out there.

29

When Your Elevator Pitch Has A Pitch Problem

Is it safe to assume that everyone in America has watched American Idol? Based on the vote tally each week during the season, I think it is a fair bet. And if you've seen the show, you've seen the caricatures that do the judging. The caricatures include hip/cool, sure/sensible, loving/kind and rude/contrarian. They play their roles pretty well, actually. As if they were reading off a script… hmmm.

One of the key things we are supposed to be listening for during American Idol is something called "pitch". According to one caricature (Randy), singers on idol can be a little "pitchy". Well, I never really looked for a specific definition for the word. So tonight as I began to think about your elevator pitch, I figured this was a pretty good time to get the definition right.

So, if you want info on pitch, where do you go? Well, here at Tim's Strategy, we went to the folks at www.singlikeapro.com Why? Wouldn't you?

The link above tells you everything you'd probably want to know about pitch. But, a short summary from the site can be found next:

"Going off pitch when singing is also called going "off key", and it means that you sing a slightly different note then you intended to. Usually, you end up hitting a note that's a little bit higher or lower then what you were aiming for.

This is called going sharp (a little too high) or flat, which is a little too low. Everyone goes off key sometimes, but some people have a hard time controlling their pitch. Of course, there are ways to correct pitch problems."

We all do our own judging when out at networking events, don't we? I know I do. I love to listen to the variety of voices and accents. I also love to hear what people actually say and wonder whether that was what they planned to say. Are they off key or just new at sharing their careers with others?

So, in this article I'd like to help you with your pitch problems. If you have them, that is. I'll tell you my top 10 keys to an effective elevator pitch. So, without further delay...

Top 10 Keys To An Effective Elevator Pitch

1. Speak up! If everyone in the room or around the table can't hear you, you've already lost. Use your outside voice when inside or outside. It helps you command the group's attention and makes a statement that what you are saying is worth hearing. And, you know what, if I can't hear your first few words, I'll stop trying too hard.

2. Look at your audience! Yes, every one of them if you can. If the group has a leader and you address all of your comments to them, well, you lost me again. Oh, and everyone else in the room who was previously open to learning about you is also off in wonderland.

3. Like to talk? Engage your filter! If the rules say 30 or 60 seconds, please don't take twice that time. It is unfair to the others especially as networking groups get larger and require more time for this part of the meeting. Even more important? You lose people after a minute and you may not even have reached your best information yet.

4. Stand up and move around! Please don't sit. Don't stand next to your seat. And once up in the front of the room, try to move around a bit. Your physical movement, like the strength of your voice, helps to send a message that you are sharing something interesting. What does it mean to move around "a bit"? Two or three steps each way is fine. If you find yourself across the room after 10 seconds, rein yourself in.

5. Pauses, small breaths and other ways to create emphasis. I've heard a few people give an elevator pitch that sounded more like a speed reading. Remember, this should be conversational. So, pause after an important point or a big accomplishment. Place emphasis on certain other points you want people to remember. Be in control of what people hear and what ends up on the floor.

6. Smile and be approachable! Being in transition does not warrant a eulogy. Your elevator pitch is not a time to be solemn, over-confident or otherwise serious. You can be confident about your skills and experience but make sure your delivery creates interest and followers. Ever heard the "how great I am" elevator pitch? Ever want to go up and introduce yourself to that person after? Me neither.

7. Offer to help others! An elevator pitch that is solely focused on your transition needs will not garner the genuine attention and interest of others. Nope. Everyone has something to offer. So make sure you include something selfless in your words.

8. Include your specific job objectives! What are you looking for in your search? If you don't provide specific and tangible objectives to your network, they will likely forget about you. Or at least forget why they thought they should remember you. How do you do this? Build the objectives into your one sheet or networking card. Also, make sure to throw out the names of a few target companies. Oh, and share your *Watchlyst* with the group. That way they can keep track of you and others much easier!

9. Be Interesting! Find a way to make your career accomplishments relevant and interesting to everyone. Avoid using industry specific jargon that only you and a few others will understand. Use brief and specific examples of what makes you different from everyone else who sat in those chairs. I am sitting here waiting for you to say something that will allow me to remember you. What are you passionate about? Really!

10. Recognize others! If you heard something interesting from another networker who spoke before you, re-emphasize it. That says to the group that you were listening earlier and have more than just your own success in mind. You may also create an opportunity for further networking with that person as the open networking portion begins. This is networking with a purpose.

Of course this discussion has been almost entirely focused on the most common format for the modern elevator speech.

You. Standing in front of 10-50 people. No elevator. And a timer (if the group is lucky).

Really this is more of an introduction, isn't it?

You are introducing yourself to the network that may be able to help you find your next job.

So here's a format for your introduction that may help. It's called *BigPitch*™ because it's just you.

In front of a big room or a big group of people...

Nice to meet you. I hope.

30

Hey, Mr. Life Of The Party. Shouldn't You Be Networking?

I was walking through Old Town in San Diego last weekend. As I sauntered (that's what you do in Old Town) along the sidewalk I ran into the gentleman who was just finishing a cigar, staring across the landscape that has become so familiar to him. Of course, he's a plaster figurine. A Mexican caballero looking for a place to have a little fun.

If you can't tell, he is a bit stuck in his ways. He can't move. It's not his fault, though. Someone put him there one day and gave him a personality, a "look", a few bad habits and, yes, a job.

His job is to deliver authenticity to the restaurant and to suggest, with a playful sincerity, the lightly sinful nature of the establishment.

As I came upon him, I knew there was a blog idea here. A way to tell a story about job search that could not be told without him. In fact, I thought about giving him a voice and letting him share the story. But he was a bit under the weather and would be hard to understand.

I'll let you name him yourself.

Poor guy is left there day and night without an ability to adjust to fashion, wipe his brow or ever really take advantage of the vices that were provided him (he carries a gun, a cigar and a bottle of tequilla). The gun probably doesn't work, the tequila is likely dry and he's been looking for a "light" for years.

He is also unable to welcome guests to the restaurant or chat up the other local businesspeople. Poor guy can't build relationships even though it would really do him some good.

What's stopping you from networking?

Now, I have not taken a poll. But my guess is that there is a substantial number of employed people who are a lot like our friend. Same job, same spot, no need to move. Why should they? They are also very likely not networking. Why should they?

I'd also be curious as to how many people, recently laid off, are now struggling to find traction in job search. Now, more than ever, job search relies upon a significant and motivated network. Motivated, that is, to help YOU. The problem is a big one, though.

So I want you to picture a friend of yours, working or looking, that is not a good networker. Specifically, they are not good because they have been lazy. Believing that the days of needing others are far, far away.

Now that you have your friend pictured, imagine them as the man in plaster above. They just found out that they were laid off. Now imagine the time it will take them to remove the bottle from the knee and the cigar from the mouth. Imagine the damage they will do to their body as the plaster crumbles and falls to the ground.

Passers by will see them struggling. Some may help while other will just stare in shock at this previously immovable object. Think of the Tin Man's first oiling by Dorothy but replace tin with plaster.

How awkward it is to try to do something for the first time. They will be clunky and slow. They will be selfish because they need something right now and don't realize that others see networking as more of a two-way street. Over time, but still two-way.

If and when your friend reaches out to you, there will be much to do. Of course you'll help him or her because you are a successful networker and know that if you help now, your help will come later.

Do me a favor, though. That friend of yours? Lend them this book and suggest they read this chapter. They could use the help.

Say: "Hey (friend) - I know you are a little new to this networking business. Please don't be like the plaster guy in this chapter. Oh, and let me know how I can help."

If you ever make it to Old Town, keep your eyes peeled for the man made of plaster. He could use a friend.

Bonus Chapters!

31

The First 5 Minutes.
How To Kick-off A
Successful Interview

I'll be honest. I can tell pretty quick whether you are likely a good fit for a job. And I can tell in the first 5 minutes.

If that sounds unfair, wrong or short-sighted then you need to remember that we are all human. And that we all react very quickly to a variety of stimuli. Many of them are ones that we cannot even identify. Just a feeling but one that stays with you all the way to the group meeting where the candidate's fate is decided.

So even if I am not consciously aware of all the stimuli, I will tell you that there are things that I am conscious of and do look for in the first 5 minutes. You know what they say about a good first impression, right?

So, whether this is exactly right or not, here's the truth from my viewpoint. As an interviewer over twenty years and as a job seeker on the other side of the desk.

1st MINUTE
Your approach is important. The way you walk and carry yourself. The way you communicate with whoever is guiding you to my office matters. I am looking for confident but not full of yourself.

Friendly but not too comfortable. If you are tentative on the way in, that's a problem. It's important that you act as if you deserve to be there.

Look nice. No frayed shirts. No twisted neck ties. Shine your shoes. New, clean coat. Should be obvious. Be hydrated. Dry mouth helps no one. The presentation of you as a candidate starts with how prepared you look. How you speak.

Your handshake says something. We all know this, right? So why are there so many bad handshakes? A confident, inviting smile tells me you are relaxed. That helps everyone else relax. Immediate and consistent eye contact. Introduce yourself to me. Now I know how to pronounce your name and you get a chance to say it with pride. It tells me you are engaged and ready. You are not sweating or breathing hard. It says you got there early and had plenty of time to check in and rest your legs.

2nd MINUTE

Say "thank you" for the opportunity and grab a seat once I do. Thank you? Sure, why not? I had a lot of people to choose from in that stack of resumes. Oh, and everybody likes to hear it. Tell me something that lets me know this is an important interview and that you are excited for the opportunity. Not desperate. Appreciative.

Engage in a little light banter before my questions begin. Have a few intro questions to lighten the moment. Allows me to see you as a possible co-worker vs. someone with whom I am jousting.

Appear comfortable. Be interested in me and in the company from the start. And also? Provide long or short answers to each question, as appropriate. Open ended questions are asked to elicit a deeper, more detailed response. Have one ready. Closed ended questions are asked to get specific details. Be ready with those, too.

3rd MINUTE

Keep eye contact. Have good posture. Says you haven't relaxed or become complacent. When in doubt, provide a shorter answer. This allows you to hit with your best points. Allowing me a follow-on as necessary. Meandering or long answers early in the interview says that you are winging it. Or that you aren't sure what I was asking. So you provide the whole truth. And then some.

Ask me to clarify a question. Ask me if an answer was satisfactory. It says, early on, that you care that I am getting the right information. And it will guide you as well.

4th MINUTE

Include key "leave behind" points in your answers. Start doing so in your response to an open ended question that gets to career summary ("Tell me about yourself"). Guide me back to successes, traits or key accomplishments. These allow me to envision your repeating those someday on my team.

Be real. Be honest. Give me the sense that you are the real person I am interviewing. Not someone who is trying desperately to fit a certain stereotype. If you get a question that forces you to admit a lack of perfect fit, admit it and move on. Don't create a new past for yourself.

5th MINUTE

Look for an opportunity to ask a follow-on question. Keeps interview conversational. Like the beginning of a solid and trusting partnership. Inquire about my challenges, team objectives and goals for the next few years. While I may not leave you an obvious hole in my questioning, look to ask one at the end of an answer to a prior question. Understand my situation and you can better position yourself to be part of the solution.

Be interesting. Make key points by inflection and emphasis. Displays focus, understanding and passion. In short, give me solid indications that you are someone with whom I should spend the entire 45-60 minutes. Make me want to get deep into your background. Tease me with an interesting story of how you creatively solved a big problem. Paint me a bright picture and get me involved. Engaged in what happened and the role you played.

Establish yourself not just as a pursuer but also as the pursued. I expect to be interviewed as well. Early and throughout. You are not taking over the interview, but rather looking for openings to gain the information you need to make a separate and independent decision about whether the company is right for you.

So...

Your first five minutes should read like the back cover of a good spy novel. Convince me there is a great story with you. That you are a great character. Well developed, interesting and driven to have a big impact. One that compels me to dig deep and read on. But don't wait too long to begin sharing some of those juicy details. Show me your best traits early and keep the measurable examples coming.

I've got a business to run and grow. And I need someone's help to do it.

Make those first 5 minutes count.

32

8 Ways To Scare Employers Away. Is This You?

Employers can be a finicky bunch. They can also be risk averse. And in this economy they are being both of these in spades. There are enough highly qualified candidates for each position to fill a large conference table. So highly qualified is now the base expectation, right?

If you are an HR person or a direct hiring manager, you are looking for ways to filter a group of applicants. To explore aspects of each candidate that will allow you to remove them from the active list. You are trying to bring a qualified panel of people who can each do the job in their own individual ways. This is one of the reasons that behavioral interviewing has become so popular.

As a job seeker, your job is to significantly limit the number of factors about you that can act as a filtering device. This should not include misrepresenting your experience or skills to move to the top of the "qualified list". But it does mean this:

Don't Be A Scarecrow

So what does that mean really? Well, you might say, "All I'm trying to do is get an audience with people who can offer me a job. If I have to get on all fours and howl to the moon to do that, well, call me a coyote".

But sometimes what you do and don't do in an effort to get attention, can often backfire. Like a loud shot that scares birds away.

So what are 8 ways to scare employers away?

1. Get cute with your cover letter. Cute can come in a variety of forms and few are rarely worth the risk. Generally they look like what they are… a way of trying too hard to get noticed.

2. Show desperation. I've before shared the perils of playing the role of the desperado. It is a dangerous game to play as it involves exposing how much you need the job and how little else you have going on in your search. So, please, don't be a desperado. Great in westerns – bad in job search.

3. Drop a resume to an employer once a week. The old "make them say no until they say yes" approach. Too many resumes too often are not a positive sign. Too many phone calls? Too many e-mails? All convey a lack of confidence. Look to be the pursued, not the pursuer.

4. Include (Your Last Name) & Associates Consulting Inc. as the present job on your resume. And when asked, express enthusiasm for the independence you feel as a consultant. Companies would like to hire people who will commit to and want to be a part of the new company for a good period of time. The risk-averse employer will see "the independent consultant" in you as a hiring risk.

5. Meander. Are you one who likes to talk? Afraid of a short, crisp answer? Well, whether you realize it or not, most interviewers want a nice short answer followed up by some supportive details. We like to hear a story, sure, but one that has

a clear point and an obvious connection to the benefit. So, if you are one who likes to talk, learn to throttle it back.

6. Wear old or tired clothes. Old twisted ties, blouses that are falling apart at the sleeve, shirts that don't fit well. Either way, it sends the wrong message. Either you are not aware that your clothes would be turned away at Goodwill or have not noticed their downward turn. Regardless. The effect on the hiring manager is the same. It all gets noticed.

7. Have a cell phone message or an e-mail address that suggests something negative or unprofessional about you. If your cell phone message includes a shout out to your brother going to college at Chico State, let's modify it for now. If your e-mail address is based on your nickname of "3 Beers Johnson", I'd either get a new nickname or get a new e-mail address from Gmail.

8. Argue with the HR department. Fiercely defend why you clearly are the most qualified for the job. In fact, act baffled as to how, after three rounds of interviews, you were not the first offer. Well, guess what, you are no longer in the running for a possible back-up offer.

Job search is an emotional roller coaster and none of us do it without a few mistakes. Just please try to avoid the big and glaring ones if you can.

Our goal is to attract people to us... not run them off.

Other books
from Tim Tyrell-Smith*

10 tools
The Tools Of Intelligent Job Search

I Can See Clearly Now
The Benefits of Taking Action on Your Ideas

*available as an ebook via timsstrategy.com

www.ingramcontent.com/pod-product-compliance
Lightning Source LLC
Chambersburg PA
CBHW051545170526
45165CB00002B/893